POWERHOUSE

The Meek School at Ole Miss

by

Ronald Farrar

YOKNAPATAWPHA PRESS
Oxford, Mississippi

Published by Yoknapatawpha Press, P.O. Box 248, Oxford, MS 38655

ISBN 978-0-916242-77-0

Jacket photograph by Katherine Williamson. Printed in the USA

To the students and faculty whose dedication and talent
are the real story of Ole Miss journalism

Contents

Getting the Story

They don't teach you how to sit in a dinky, one-seat crop duster in Journalism 101. Not exactly sit. Hunker. More like perching on a gas tank behind the pilot, bracing your legs and hoping for the best as a cloud of weevil-killing chemicals spews behind you, zooming back and forth over a cotton field, both hands holding onto your camera for dear life as you try to get some good steady shots. For that matter, nobody taught Elizabeth Vowell how to sweet-talk the pilot into letting her on the plane to begin with. But what this senior in journalism at Ole Miss did learn was how to tell a story, and how to listen when her gut told her that without this God's view of the Delta country, she didn't have enough to tell it right.

Vowell and seven other J-school students were there as part of an in-depth investigation they called the Delta Project. Led by two faculty members—one a former national editor at the *Miami Herald*, the other a former editor at the *San Jose Mercury News*—the students had studied the Mississippi Delta in the classroom for weeks before they went there. Then they'd spent the last week talking to dozens of people, breathing in cigarette smoke and listening to the blues where the blues first sprang up, in run-down honky tonks around Clarksdale.

"But we sensed that the only way to get a feel for the entire region was from the air," Vowell said. A male student went to the farmhouse beside a crop duster plane's hangar and asked the owner for permission to ride along. He said no. Vowell went back on her own. "You're gonna think I'm crazy," she told the man, "but we want a shot of the whole area." She talked some more, and she got the shot. "I worked my butt off to get it," she recalls.

The view was gorgeous. Vowell could see where they'd been, the little towns strung along the Mississippi River. They seemed to her connected in some way, yet so isolated. She saw the humble Moon Lake churches where some of the people she'd talked to had gotten baptized, and the little cemeteries where their dead were buried, in the rich, black earth that had sustained and challenged them all their lives. She might have seen more, except she was looking through the camera's viewfinder the whole time. Even so, she recognized the Delta "as a world unto its own." Afterward, the pilot relented and took up some of the other students. They saw the Delta the same way.

A native of Quitman, Miss., Vowell had never been immersed in the Delta. The Delta project team was assigned to produce a magazine and a CD as well as a documentary program for television. The magazine won the prestigious Robert F. Kennedy Journalism Award, honoring it as the best student magazine journalism produced in the nation that year.

She and her team are part of a long line of plucky, talented young men and women who have studied journalism at Ole Miss and then gone on to outstanding careers in communications. It is students like these, and the veteran journalists who taught them, who have given the Edwin and Becky Meek School of Journalism and New Media at the University of Mississippi the tradition it has today.

Brady Hall (photo by Kathy Ferguson)

Where It All Began

A small-town weekly newspaper editor in Columbia, MO, Walter Williams, eventually succeeded where Joseph Pulitzer and others had not. Williams was active in various newspaper associations, and through them he had traveled widely, visiting newspaper offices across the United States and abroad. The more papers he visited, the more convinced he became that too many journalists simply were not respected. And convinced, too, that maybe their performance didn't deserve respect. In a forthright message to his fellow editors, Williams wrote:

> The careful reader of the newspapers cannot fail to notice the errors.... Not errors of fact, but errors due to ignorance of history, geography, political economy, grammar, and other branches of learning. These mistakes are not confined to any one class or condition of journals. They are found in country and city publications, in the writings of the reporter, the telegraph editor and the editor-in-chief. One purpose of a school of journalism would be to direct the thought and studies of the student along the lines that would be useful... in avoiding such errors.

Williams thought the University of Missouri, situated in his hometown of Columbia, could provide the ideal setting for the type of journalism school he envisioned. His proposal, however, was quickly rejected by the general faculty. Even some prominent newspaper people thought that a school of journalism had no place on a university campus. One of them put it this way:

> I do not agree with you (Walter Williams). . .It is the fixed conviction of every one of us (journalists) that we are, like the poets, "born, not made;" moreover, every journalist holds that when he was born, the seed gave out.

A smallish, soft-spoken man, Williams was also determined and, perhaps more significant, politically savvy. Rather than fight the academy, he decided to sidestep it. He managed to get appointed to the University of Missouri Board of Curators (trustees), and in that capacity became a close friend and ally of the university's president, Dr. Richard Jesse. Soon he was, in fact, the driving force among the curators and President Jesse relied upon him more and more. A few years later, Jesse's health had declined and he planned to step down. One of his last acts, in 1905, was to reward his close friend Walter Williams by persuading the curators to establish a school of journalism.

That much settled, the next objective was to find a dean. Offers went out to several nationally prominent journalists. One by one, they turned down the job, regarding it as a risky, speculative venture into uncharted territory. After more than a year of refusals, the curators turned to Williams, urging him to resign his newspaper editorship and take the deanship himself. Though he had long fought to gain acceptance for the idea of a school, he was hesitant to become a dean because, as he told his fellow curators, his academic credentials were practically nonexistent: Not only had he never had been to college, he had never finished high school. But whatever his academic shortcomings may have been, there was no doubt of his intellect, his leadership skills, his energy and his enthusiasm. He accepted the deanship.

When the world's first School of Journalism did open at Missouri in 1908, the president of the university, A. Ross Hill, spoke to the assembled faculty, outlining some of his goals and aspirations. In that well-crafted address, there was this graceful, prophetic passage welcoming the new School of Journalism into the fold:

> The University of Missouri is the first in America to establish and organize a School of Journalism. I believe it is possible for this School to give dignity to the profession of journalism, to anticipate to some extent the difficulties that journalism must meet and to prepare its graduates to overcome them; to give prospective journalists a professional spirit and high ideals of service; to discover those with real talent for the work in the profession, and to discourage those who are likely to prove failures in the profession, and to give the State better newspapers and a better citizenship. I hope the faculty of the School of Journalism, upon whom rests the responsibility for all this, will prove worthy of the trust imposed in them.

The new School of Journalism generated a great deal of favorable publicity in newspapers throughout the nation, and soon other colleges and universities picked up the idea. By 1912, some 32 journalism programs were known to exist. Mostly these were in the Midwest. Louisiana State University and North Carolina had the only journalism programs in the South.

Hotty Toddy

"You Never Graduate from Ole Miss"

For much of its history, the University of Mississippi—Ole Miss— rarely got in a rush. Its relaxed, unhurried pace was sometimes difficult for newcomers to fathom. One eager young department chairman, who'd arrived on campus only a week before, had already fired off half a dozen memos to the Lyceum, campus headquarters of the top administrators. He soon got a telephone call from one of the university's vice chancellors.

"Slow down, son, you're at Ole Miss now," he said, not unkindly, in his thick Southern drawl. "Which means that if you send in a requisition for a new desk—well, sooner or later somebody *might* go out and chop down a tree."[1]

The laid-back atmosphere of Ole Miss was reflected in the surrounding community of Oxford. Or maybe it was the other way around. A comfortable, friendly small town built around a courthouse square, Oxford had been founded in 1837 on land bought from the Chickasaw tribe. It was named after the famous university city in England, and almost from the outset its citizens energetically campaigned to establish a college, the University of Mississippi, in their town. In 1848, they got their wish. But just a few years after that promising start, Mississippi seceded from the Union and virtually all of the able-bodied students left the campus to enlist in the Confederate army. The university's chancellor begged the students to stay on and complete their education, as did the Confederacy president, Jefferson Davis. Sending young lads off to war, Davis said, was "grinding the seeds of the republic."[2] The university was officially shut down during the war, its buildings converted to a hospital. Many of the university's students would be killed or wounded or captured. In 1864, Union forces stormed through Northern Mississippi, leaving Oxford and the college in ruins.

The courthouse was rebuilt in 1872, and in time the stores around the square began to reappear. Because Oxford is situated in the northern, thinly populated area of a mostly rural state, the town's growth came slowly. But it was, and is, a lovely, yet strangely complex, place. The town's most famous citizen, the Nobel award-winning novelist, William Faulkner, said of it in 1955:

> I discovered that my own little postage stamp of native

soil was worth writing about and that I would never live long enough to exhaust it, and that by sublimating the actual into the apocryphal I would have complete liberty to use whatever talent I might have to its absolute top. It opened up a gold mine of other people, so I created a cosmos of my own.[3]

If Oxford was and is special, the same could be said for the University of Mississippi, whose campus seems to infuse an enduring warmth and affection. "You can earn a degree from the University of Mississippi," goes a popular saying, "but you never graduate from Ole Miss."

1960: Larry Speakes, left, with Stan Dearman, editor of *The Mississippian,* and Robert Clifft, business manager.

In 2011, a visiting writer from *The New York Times* found himself caught up in the atmosphere of Oxford[4] and Ole Miss, an aura he called "parties, prose, and football." The prose reference goes well beyond the legacy of William Faulkner: An astonishing number of famous authors lived and wrote in Oxford[4] and the three bookstores on Oxford's town square do a bustling business. "Civilization and distillation are revered here," he wrote, quoting Faulkner, "and, strangely, nowhere are these more in evidence than a football Saturday when the Ole Miss Rebels are at home. The magnificent Grove, situated in front of the Lyceum, is temporarily covered by a sea of tents, populated by literally thousands of tailgaters merrily fortifying themselves for

12

an afternoon or evening of football. "It is, as *The Times* writer described it, "a kind of refined, khaki-wearing Mardi Gras" where, he added, "otherwise sane adults are unembarrassed every ten minutes or so to scream out:

> Hotty toddy, Gosh almighty
> Who the hell are we? Hey!
> Flim flam, Bim bam
> OLE MISS BY DAMN![5]

If the Michelin Guide rated tailgate experiences, the Grove at Ole Miss would be awarded five stars. But "Hotty Toddy" is more than a rowdy, joyous, unforgettable tradition. It is an affirmation.

Like Oxford, the university evolved gradually. Hardly surprising, then, that when Ole Miss got around to establishing a Department of Journalism in 1947, other institutions had already been at it for years.

The University of Missouri was the pioneer, opening the world's first school of journalism in 1908. When Joseph Pulitzer, then arguably the most distinguished newspaper publisher in America, tried to persuade Columbia University in New York to offer courses in journalism—and he would give Columbia several millions to pay for it—he was rebuffed. "We don't teach bricklaying or carpentry or plumbing," Pulitzer was told in effect, "and we won't teach journalism."

The world's first School of Journalism—at the University of Missouri—managed to open any way, in 1908. It generated a great deal of favorable publicity in newspapers throughout the nation, and soon other colleges and universities picked up the idea. By 1912, some 32 journalism programs were known to exist.

The popularity and rapid growth of journalism schools provoked little interest to the top administrators at the University of Mississippi, however. The campus was small, fewer than 2,000 students, and the emphasis at Ole Miss was on liberal arts; that and on preserving traditions. "From the beginning," as one insightful historian put it, "Mississippi's wealthy planters and elite lawyers dominated the board of trustees and imposed their values on the institution. The central purpose of their university was not to introduce students to new and exciting ideas but to perpetuate conformity to established ones."[6] An irate resident of the Mississippi Delta, Walter Clark, wrote in 1917 that, "The university for many years has been the plaything of politics." [7] This meant, among much else, that new ideas—from racial integration to establishment of additional graduate and professional programs, such as journalism, on the campus—would not be encouraged.

Besides, there was already a student newspaper, *The Mississippian*, begun in 1911 and staffed primarily by English majors and anybody else who wanted to contribute.[8] Though there was a Publications Board, comprised mostly of faculty and administrators, it did not censor the newspaper. Essentially, *The Mississippian* was more of a social club than a training ground for professional journalists. On occasion, the English department might teach a course somewhat related to journalism. Some students wanted much more than this.[9]

Just after World War II, Ole Miss began to change. Returning veterans created a surge in enrollment, and with it came a demand for more courses and degree programs. A new chancellor, Dr. J. D. Williams, was determined to upgrade the facilities ("they are that of an undernourished junior college") and, significantly, to elevate Ole Miss from what he called "a finishing school for the children of the gentry."[10]

His timing was ideal to expand academic and professional opportunities for students and faculty. One such program, Williams decided, should be in journalism. He envisioned a modest beginning, a small department, but of high quality. Williams convinced the trustees to make it happen. Then he set about finding a good man to run it.

Gerald Forbes

The Founder

Dr. Gerald Forbes, chair, Department of Journalism, 1947-56.

Once Ole Miss decided to create a Department of Journalism, the next step was figuring out where to put it. Liberal arts was the dominant college, but journalism was perceived to be a bit too tradesman-like to be thrust into the lofty regions occupied by English and history and philosophy. The School of Business faculty members were less opposed to the new department, so the chancellor decided to place it there.[11] He and the business dean, Horace Brown, took applications for the new position of Chairman of the Department of Journalism.

One of those invited to the campus for interviews was Dr. Charles G. Forbes, then on the history faculty at Oklahoma State University.

Gerald Forbes had been an English major at the University of Oklahoma until he dropped out to marry his high school sweetheart. Later, he went back to finish his bachelor's degree, then earned a master's and a doctorate in history. He planned to be a university professor, but chose to get some journalism experience first. He spent 10 years on various weekly and daily newspapers, including the *Daily Oklahoman* (Oklahoma City), the Dallas *Times-Herald*, and the Fort Worth *Star-Telegram*.[12] During World War II he served as an officer in the Army Air Corps, after which he was hired by Oklahoma A & M (now Oklahoma State University) and was quickly promoted to associate professor of History. Then he heard about the new opening at Ole Miss. An opportunity to establish and run his own journalism program was irresistible, and he jumped at it.

During his interviews with the chancellor and Dean Brown, he was asked what the new department should be and do. That must have been an interesting moment: Neither the chancellor nor the business dean had any experience with journalism, so neither man could be sure just what questions to ask, much less what answers to hope for. Forbes had not been interviewed for a chairmanship before and wasn't sure just how much he could deliver. He decided to punt, asking for time to ponder the matter. When he got back to Oklahoma, he would recall some years later, "I wrote down two or three pages of anything I could think of to make the department grow and mailed the list back to Oxford." The letter soon was followed by a telephone call from dean Brown, congratulating him on his ideas and offering him the job.[13]

1972: Otis Tims, *Daily Mississippian* news editor; Sparky Reardon, front page editor; and Patsy Brumfield, executive editor.

When the Department officially began, in February1947, it was assigned a tiny space in the Lyceum. A few months later, it was moved to two classrooms and two offices in "Temporary A," one of four war surplus buildings situated near Bishop Hall, not far from the Lyceum. "Temporary A" was an ugly frame building, military barracks style, painted gray and with an asphalt roof. The classrooms were small and the office space smaller still. There was no air conditioning. This was considered a stopgap measure, but the department would remain there for more than a decade.[14]

Some 79 students signed up for journalism courses, immediately making the new department one of the larger ones on campus. Forbes did the teaching himself. The curriculum was built around the reporting and editing classes. The Ole Miss course catalog listed an ambitious set of additional offerings, however: Management of the Weekly Newspaper; Principles of Advertising; Layout and Copy Writing; News Photography; History of Journalism; Magazine Editing; Circulation Problems; Feature Writing; Special Articles; Public Opinion and the Press; The Press and Contemporary Thought, and Editorial Direction.[15]

Not all of these were offered in any given semester, for no one man could teach them all. He would be authorized an additional faculty position, and he held it open for Samuel Talbert, a promising young Southerner who was teaching at Lehigh University while working on his doctoral dissertation at the University of Iowa. It isn't clear just how Forbes knew about Sam Talbert, but obviously the hire proved to be a crucial one.

1971: *Daily Mississippian* sports staff included Buddy Bynum, Tim Kriehn and Dudley Marble.

During his job interviews, Forbes and Chancellor Williams agreed that the Department of Journalism would not directly influence the student newspaper, *The Mississippian*. The university had never deviated from its belief that the student newspaper should be free from faculty or administrative control. Editorial policy aside, however, *The Mississippian* was chronically short on news copy, and Forbes had students who could generate lots of it. So Forbes offered articles produced by his reporting students to the student editors of *The Mississippian*, who were free to use them or not use them. Usually, the articles were welcomed. It was a win-win situation for Forbes: His students gained the experience (and the clippings for their folios) from seeing their work in print, and the news coverage of *The Mississippian* was expanded and improved—all without any loss of freedom by the student editors.

1973: *Daily Mississippian* staff, Becky Mauney, news editor; Scott Ware, sports editor; Nancy Tipton, wire editor.

Energetic and plainspoken, Forbes worked heroically to make his new, one-man department succeed. In addition to handling a brutal teaching load, Forbes also in his first year managed to:

- Get his reporting students to write articles for their hometown newspapers. The first-year production alone was some 40 columns, or about 800 column inches, of copy that generated publicity for the university as well as clippings for the students.
- Organize a Press Club, which became a forerunner of the Ole Miss chapter of the national societies for journalism students and professionals in the field.
- Brought in as "get acquainted" guest speakers some 15 editors and publishers from throughout the region. From its beginning, journalism at Ole Miss enjoyed a close and mutually respectful affiliation with the Mississippi Press Association.
- Put on a two-day Editors' Short Course on the campus, which drew 100 Mississippi professionals. The guest speakers included Mark Ethridge, publisher of the Louisville *Courier-Journal*, and George McLean, publisher of the *Tupelo Journal*, along with various other accomplished practitioners in photography and advertising and circulation.
- And, perhaps most important to Gerald Forbes, he established the Mississippi Scholastic Press Institute to expose high school students to journalism at Ole Miss. Nearly 150 students and teachers attended the MSPI's first two-day event in late Spring, 1947.[16]

This was a singular triumph for him. Back when he was preparing an outline for the chancellor and the dean of his aspirations for the new department, the first item on his list was a yearly short course for high school students "on putting out a newspaper." He reasoned that some of the best and brightest high school students might be interested in studying journalism at college, preferably at Ole Miss. Forbes never lost his belief in, and affection for, the scholastic press.[17]

Politicians are said to believe that their first, and most overwhelming, priority is to get re-elected. Chairmen of new academic departments face a comparable mission —survival. With every decision he made, Gerald Forbes broke new ground. He was determined to create and build, but given few resources with which to do it. And to establish a professional program on a campus where traditions and the prevailing culture made it easy for him to fail. He did not fail.

The momentum Forbes generated during that critical first year was sustained, and even accelerated, after that. Enrollment increased by 10 percent the following fall semester, and by 20 percent the following spring. Attendance of high school students to the Scholastic Press Institute nearly doubled. The Press Club that Forbes organized would eventually qualify students for membership in two national organizations, Sigma Delta Chi for men and Theta Sigma Phi for women. With the financial support of *The Mississippian*, he got a darkroom set up—in a tiny closet, actually. Forbes had even gained enough confidence to ask the administration for a reading room. He had somehow wrangled free subscriptions to 20 state and regional newspapers, and had been allotted $400 to buy books, which had to be stored on a shelf in the department office.

He also pointed out in his annual report that "Accreditation is desirable and will be sought as soon as it is feasible."[18]

While a reading room of sorts would come the next year, national accreditation remained unattainable, a goal for the distant future. Even so, the rest of the campus had to know that this new Department of Journalism was neither timid nor lacking in its ambition.

1970: Theta Sigma Phi Officers (l-r) Susan Langdon, Pat Strickland, Nan Russell and Terry Price on porch swing at Brady Hall.

For all his intense devotion to his department and to journalism, Forbes refused to take himself seriously. One of his first students remembered him this way:

> Forbes insisted on being addressed as "Mister" Forbes and not "Doctor" Forbes. He was adamant about this. His teaching style was informal: he would sit on or lean against a table rather than stand behind a lectern. The chairman would sometimes sit on his hands on the rim of the old *Mississippian* copy desk. He wore rimless spectacles and had only a few strands of hair on his head. When amused, Forbes would throw back his head and let out a loud, cackling laugh.[19]

He was a wiry man, of medium build and perhaps five feet, seven inches in height. He wore a coat and tie to work, but soon shed the jacket.

Usually relaxed and informal in class, Forbes could erupt into profanity—mostly just for shock effect, one student remembers. As one day in the old Temp A with no air conditioning, when the DDT truck arrived to spray under the building. "God damn, let's get out of here," he shouted. "They're trying to kill us!"[20]

Forbes hosted many social gatherings at his home, held wiener roasts in the woods behind fraternity row, sponsored social organizations for his students, helping them bond with each other and, more importantly, to talk beyond the classroom about contemporary issues and job opportunities. These clubs also boosted student aspirations to crack the journalism job market. He had learned, perhaps in the Army, the value of building *esprit de corps* and professional pride.

Dr. Gerald Forbes, Liz Shiver and Will Norton at the 75th anniversary of the founding of the *Mississippian*. Forbes was the first chairman of the Ole Miss Department of Journalism, Liz Shiver a former *Mississippian* editor, and Will Norton, chair of the Department of Journalism. (*Oxford Eagle*, April 10, 1986.)

"Forbes was a wonderful and irascible character who taught us only two things that I really remember," recalls one of his first students, Liz Shiver. "First, never use clichés (such as 'fraught with difficulties') and never be intimidated to question anyone…. Most of us also look back in amazement at the sense of confidence he instilled in us, especially given how little we actually knew."[21]

"Dr. Forbes did not believe in exams," recalls Martha van Bibber Kelley, ('55). "He knew from experience that a journalist must be skilled enough to sell his or her work. To pass his class, we students had to sell some of what we wrote. I sold mine by stringing for the (Memphis) *Commercial Appeal,* and I also sold a feature story to the (New Orleans) *Times Picayune*, a small portion

22

of which was picked up by *Time* magazine. Can you imagine how thrilled I was?"[22]

September 1948 marked the beginning of the department's second year—and the addition of a sorely needed second faculty member.

```
                                          Box 7
                                          University, Mississippi
                                          May 31, 1948


My dear Talbert

I must ask you to forgive  this paper, but I'm in a hurry
to get this letter off to you and I don't want to make a
trip to the office on that account.

I have just returned from a conference with  Dean Brown
regarding you, and we are equally enthusiastic regarding
the proposition of  offering you the position in the
Department of Journalism.  I had hoped this letter could
contain such an offer.

But  the situation regarding the budget prevents any
definite statement at this moment.  The situation is this.
The budget for the next two years is in the hands of the
Board of Regents for Higher Institutions.  The Board
will meet  in two days (Wednesday) and then Thursday we'll
know what the figures are.

I requested a salary of $4,000, but I don't know what the
Board will do to it. I think it will be cut some, but
only God  could guess exactly what will come out. I feel
certain   that the salary for nine months will be well up
for the rank of Assistant Professor.

Thursday I expect to make you a definite offer, when I
will  know just  what the job will pay.

The Dean and I discussed the  prospects of an apartment
for you and your family, and we feel  sure that we can
arrange for a place to stay.  Several of the buildings
have been reserved for faculty, and I think about twenty
such families  live in them --- generally, congenial
young couples with  a youngster or two. The idea was that
we would rent one, and sublet it  for the summer so
that it would be available for you to move into perhaps
in August.

This is just to keep you posted, and you'll hear again
from me Thursday.

                              Sincerely,


                              Gerald Forbes

Mr. Samuel S. Talbert
Lehigh University
Bethlehem, Penna.
```

Sam Talbert had now completed his doctorate in mass communications at the University of Iowa. Iowa had pioneered doctoral education in this field and is considered to have conferred the first Ph.D. in mass communications. (It went to Dr. George F. Gallup, later to establish the famed, highly respected Gallup Poll organization.) While still a graduate student at Iowa, Talbert had been noticed and recruited. But Talbert, a Southerner by birth as well as temperament, came to Ole Miss, where he was destined to play a major role in the development of that journalism program.

With Talbert now on board, the department gained additional academic stature. Forbes had an earned doctorate, but it was in history. Talbert's Ph.D. was in mass communications, seemingly more fitting for a journalism program, and all the more esteemed because of its rarity: At that time, only about 20 doctorates in mass communication had been conferred. Student enrollment continued to build; the two-year-old department had already become the ninth largest on the Ole Miss campus. And it was the only journalism program in Mississippi.

It was time, Forbes thought, to seek national accreditation from the American Council on Education for Journalism. Only about 40 journalism programs in the nation had qualified for ACEJ accreditation at that time. The standards were high, and the pre-accreditation scrutiny was rigorous. Nevertheless, Forbes made his case to Chancellor Williams, who agreed that outside consultants should look at the program. But this preliminary survey of the program produced little hope that accreditation would be realized. The department's tiny budget was given as the primary reason.[23]

National accreditation would eventually be awarded, but Gerald Forbes would not be around to see it. Despite the growth, in student enrollment and in respect throughout the state, Forbes decided he had had enough. On July 16, 1956, he resigned.

His personnel file, maintained by what is now called the Human Resources Department, lists his reason for leaving as "To accept a position at Northeastern State College, Tahlequah, Oklahoma." But this was amended a few days later: "Mrs. Forbes called and asked that this be changed to Department of Journalism, San Jose State College, San Jose, California" and left a new forwarding address, one in San Jose.

California's privacy regulations, which verge on the neurotic, prevent revealing whether Dr. Forbes ever taught at San Jose State, and if so, for how long.

But why, after launching a journalism program, and loving it and nurturing it along, with considerable success for nine years, did Forbes leave Ole Miss? In the absence of a public explanation by Forbes, returning students advanced several theories to explain what was to them a mysterious departure.

One was that he had become so captivated with photography—and he was, according to those familiar with his work, a world-class photographer—that he had decided to devote his full-time efforts to it. Those who knew him spoke of his frustration, not only with teaching and administrative duties but also with the tiny and inadequate darkroom facilities available to journalism. (That cut both ways; some students were known to complain that they couldn't develop their own photo assignments because Dr. Forbes tied up the darkroom.[24])

Another theory was that Dr. Forbes' grueling teaching and administrative load, and more or less continuous struggles of trying to make do with an utterly inadequate budget, had turned him into a burnout case. Thirty years after his resignation, in a conversation with Dr. Will Norton, then department chairman, Dr. Forbes confirmed it.[25]

Gerald Forbes' intention to leave Ole Miss must have been a shock to Sam Talbert. They were friends and colleagues in a two-person department. It was not in Gerald Forbes' character to leave a friend and colleague with no one to teach four additional scheduled courses, the continuation of departmental initiatives, and the administrative work of chairman. Talbert wrote Jere Hoar on April 29, 1956: "As you might have heard from your parents, Dr. Forbes is leaving Ole Miss and it looks like I will be taking on his chores. There is no question about the job here being open if you want it...."[26] He added, "I would like to hear from you as quickly as you can gather your thoughts on the subject."[ ]

As a man with a large family, Dr. Sam had to consider his options. Could he find a safe place to land if he decided to leave, too? He put out job inquiries. The academic search and hiring process is a slow one. If he decided to stay, could he hire the assistant professor he wanted, or one equally well qualified? He wanted someone with professional experience and a doctorate in mass communications or journalism—or, sure to receive one. All he had to offer to a top-of-the-market applicant was a paltry $4500 for nine months with summer teaching unlikely.

The Department of Journalism's existence was in the balance. If it lost both Gerald Forbes and Sam Talbert there would be no department.

Talbert did find a safe place to land, a very good one.

On May 10 he wrote that he had reached a final decision only that morning to reject a "dream job" offer from the University of Minnesota.[27]

He renewed his offer to Jere Hoar in the same letter, and relayed guarded approval from the director of the Iowa Ph.D. mass communications program. Well acquainted with professor Les Moeller, Hoar considered the recommendation lukewarm.[28]

Two days later Talbert wrote again: "I have talked with Dr. Alton Bryant (the vice chancellor for academic affairs at Ole Miss) about the possibility of hiring you for the vacancy. He is very pleased about the idea—in fact, he suggested that I get in touch with you before I mentioned that I had."

Whether Gerald Forbes participated directly in the exchange of letters is not known. Two letters, Forbes to Hoar, are missing.[29]

The big question was settled. The department would continue to exist in the immediate future because Dr. Sam had chosen to remain as chairman. With Jere Hoar's decision to cast his lot with Dr. Talbert, both faculty positions would be capably filled when classes began fall semester, 1956-1957.

Then the founder submitted his resignation.

A nagging question remains. Was the date of the Forbes resignation (July 16) coincidental, or was it a timed wrap-up to the tumultuous events he'd set in motion? Apparently, no one asked him. In his forthright way Gerald Forbes would have answered the question.

Though far away—he eventually moved to Austin, Texas—Forbes kept in touch with a few of his former students, particularly Jesse Phillips, publisher of *The Oxford Eagle*. Mostly their letters concerned family matters, but Forbes remained at heart a journalism professor: "Don't let a few free weeklies and giveaway papers win," he advised Phillips, who was at the time facing competition for advertising in the small market of Oxford. "They will not. All you have to do is sit tight, remain calm. Don't get into any scrap or hot argument with your opponent, and you'll wake up one day in a stronger position than you thought was possible."[30]

Although he had thought at one time about moving back to Oxford, he seldom returned to the Ole Miss campus. One such visit came in 1986, for the 75th anniversary of the founding of *The Daily Mississippian*. It was a joyous occasion for Forbes, by now well into his 80s, and he hardly recognized the journalism program he had invented so many years earlier.

Not long after that, he announced a gift of $100,000 to the Department of Journalism—a gigantic sum for a man whose teaching salary had been so modest. Almost immediately thereafter, however, both Dr. Forbes and his wife suffered major health problems. As their doctor and hospital bills continued to mount, the Foundation at Ole Miss quietly returned the money. On July 11, 1988, Gerald Forbes died.

When he single-handedly launched the journalism program at Ole Miss in 1947, there was no reason on earth to believe the program would ever become so successful. Yet maybe, at some level, Forbes was confident that it would. He seemed to know things like that.

Samuel S. Talbert

Dr. Sam

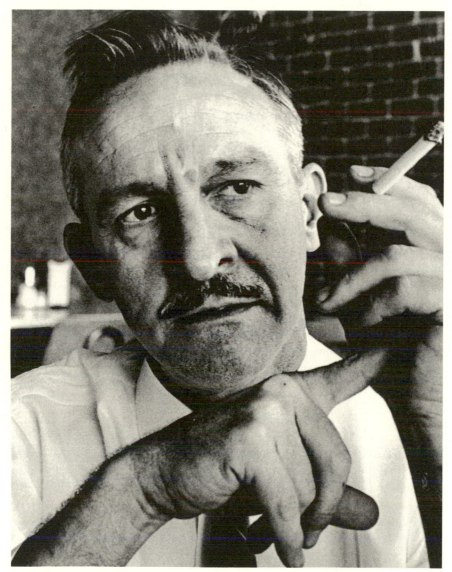

Dr. Sam Talbert, chair, Department of Journalism, 1956-72.

When Dr. Gerald Forbes started the Department of Journalism at Ole Miss, he quickly realized he needed another faculty member to handle the influx of students, many returning WWII veterans. He convinced the administration in 1948 to hire Samuel Talbert, who was teaching at Lehigh University, and writing for Pennsylvania newspapers.

Talbert, who had earned the first masters degree of journalism from the University of Florida, brought with him to Ole Miss extensive newspaper experience, expertise in advertising and in writing, editing, management and photography. He complemented Forbes' warmth and enthusiasm. Talbert's love for teaching, deep concern for all his students and ability to inspire so many of them commanded respect to the extent that, in time, "Dr. Sam" would become synonymous with journalism at Ole Miss.

After his first year of teaching, Talbert was granted an official leave of absence to work on a doctorate in mass communications at the University of Iowa, only the second such degree to have been granted at that time. In 1952, Talbert returned to Ole Miss with a PhD with the understanding that Forbes wanted Talbert to succeed him when Forbes moved on in 1956.

Hal DeCell, publisher of the *Deer Creek Pilot* of Rolling Fork, Miss. wrote in 1972, "Journalism at Ole Miss had just been established (when Talbert arrived). Under Sam's guidance it reached the recognition of being one of the best in the South."

Samuel Stubbs Talbert was born May 6, 1917, in Brinson, Ga. He earned his B.A. and M.A. at the University of Florida, and along the way he held down newspaper jobs as editor of the Warm Springs, Ga., *Mirror* and *University News* at the University of Florida. He would continue to write for newspapers throughout his career.

In 1941, when war seemed imminent, he enlisted in the Navy, eventually becoming a lieutenant commander. He served on the carrier USS Cabot in the Pacific. The ship was frequently in combat, and the noise of battle all but deafened him. His hearing problems would present him with difficulties in teaching that only a resourceful man could handle. Conversations with students and faculty became shouting matches, though amiable ones. Often his students, who adored him, would talk freely to each other during his classes, causing him to wonder what "the buzz in this room is." Occasionally, students might tease him by simply moving their lips soundlessly in answer to a question, prompting him to throw off his hearing aids and mutter "the damned things don't work." Surgery restored his hearing. Afterwards, he would quietly remind students and faculty that he could hear.[31]

Advertising was one of Talbert's main areas of expertise. After WWII, while earning his M.A. in 1946-47, he helped set up courses in advertising for the Department of Journalism at the University of Florida. A large part of his graduate work dealt with advertising problems in weekly and small daily newspapers. He wrote a booklet in connection with this study that was adopted by several universities. Later at Lehigh University he supervised the advertising department of the campus radio station and semi-weekly newspaper.

While teaching at Lehigh, Talbert co-founded a magazine called *American Opinion*. In a news release he wrote, "Critics of the American press hold that one of the chief blocks to free expression has been the failure of our mass communication media to give adequate voice to private individuals and minority groups." The magazine's purpose was to provide a forum for the exchange of ideas and freedom of expression. This was the start of an extended period of published writings.

Dr. Sam was a dark-haired, handsome man of medium height and weight. He was generally quiet and, unless riled up about something, spoke softly with an accent distinctly South Georgia. He was also a man of varied interests and considerable intellectual depth. While at Ole Miss, he wrote a number of articles for scholarly and professional journals. By 1964 his academic vita cited 104 articles. He also self-published two books: *Case Studies in Local Advertising* and *Reaching Alumni*.

His approach to teaching emphasized experience and might shock some purists whose knowledge begins and ends with a Teaching Methods class offered by a School of Education. "It doesn't make much difference about textbooks," he wrote to Jere Hoar, who was soon to join the faculty. "All of them in a particular field are virtually the same. Offhand, I don't remember the ones we have been using. I think maybe I sent a list to the bookstores some time back. I'll check on that."[32]

Talbert, however, did know the young men and women in his classes well, and he cared a great deal about each of them. One of his students in 1958, Henry Ahrens Petersen, did poorly on a test and dreaded coming to the next class meeting. But instead of the scolding he expected from his professor, Peterson recalled, Dr. Talbert said, 'Hell, Henry, you know this stuff. I'll just give you a B." Petersen obviously did know his stuff: He got a job on a magazine in New York, one owned by Dunn & Bradstreet, and worked his way through the ranks to become publisher. "Dr. Sam Talbert made me feel I was 'special,'" he would write later. "Thank God I never got over it."[33]

In addition to his academic load, Talbert's creative drive led him to write three plays and a novel, *The Amateur*, adapted as a drama and performed at Ole Miss. From 1957 until his death, he wrote a weekly column of folksy advice, "Local Business," that was sold to editors for a dollar a week. It was carried by as many as 250 newspapers. Under the "Academy Press" label he published two theses written by journalism graduate students, Emelda Capati from the Philippines and future Ole Miss journalism benefactor Ed Meek, on the subjects of pioneers who edited newspapers in Oxford. A booklet he wrote to help newspapers teach merchants the value of advertising, *How to Sell Mousetraps*, sold more than 200,000 copies and also appeared in Spanish and

Portuguese translations.

Though the journalism department was relatively small in the early years, over the 23 years Talbert was with the department, it grew in a multitude of ways: gaining national recognition and respect, more faculty, more students, a diverse curriculum, graduate level courses, many experiential opportunities for students both at Ole Miss and at the high school level, and even an expanded physical presence in a new building.

Under Talbert's chairmanship faculty began to be added, first with the hiring of Jere Hoar, followed shortly by Gale Denley. In the later years of Talbert's tenure Walter Hurt, Lee White and Neil Woodruff, among others, joined the faculty along with several graduate assistants. Talbert believed his students should have an education as close as possible to the real world of a working journalist, a factor in hiring Denley, who remained a small-town newspaper editor throughout his time at Ole Miss. To Dr. Talbert real news experience reaffirmed and reinforced academic training.

A landmark event for the department was the move in 1960 from the wooden barracks that stood near where Bishop Hall now stands to the historic Brady Hall, located in the middle of the campus near the Grove. Brady Hall had originally been built as a hospital for the University Medical School and later housed the music department. During the 1960s and early 1970s it hummed with the energy of student journalists at work. In order to house the Department of Journalism, the building was renovated to include classrooms but also a working newsroom, including a circular copy desk, dark room and printing press. On the front porch, a wooden swing provided a homey touch.

Another special feature on the porch was a printing press donated in 1960 by Gale Denley's uncle, Gerald D. Denley, publisher of the *Coffeeville Courier*. When visiting the Courier office Sam Talbert became intrigued by the George Washington hand press, c. 1850. "We gave it to him," wrote Gerald Denley, "to carry back to the Ole Miss Journalism Department where it now stands as a reminder of the olden days of printing."

1977: Will Norton, assistant professor; Ronald T. Farrar, professor and chair of the Department of Journalism; S. Gale Denley, assistant professor; Peter Barecchia, assistant professor, and Jere Hoar, professor.

Still, though a major improvement, Brady Hall was far from perfect. As Leslie Banahan ('76) put it, "While Brady Hall wasn't much of a facility, with holes in the floors, cracked tiles, dirty walls and the distinct smell of the press room and dark room, there was a sense of camaraderie and belonging that made it a great place to learn. Professors' doors were open, typewriters could be heard throughout the hallways, and the informal nature of the small building lent itself to conversation and learning."[34]

The building was fast becoming a press center, a real world news experience for students. There was no more significant moment in Brady Hall's history than during the 1962 riot, when the journalism department became an island of reason and calm while a storm raged outside its doors. On Sept. 30, 1962, when student protests over James Meredith's admission to the university spiraled into a full-blown riot, Sam Talbert remained on campus attending faculty meetings and helping to restore order. His son, Mike, recalls his father's working into the night to direct publication of a special issue of the *Mississippian* that earned student editor Sidna Brower a Pulitzer Prize nomination:

The Sunday that the riot first broke out my father was on campus all day long in meetings with university officials. We didn't see him until that afternoon, though our home was just off campus on a back street entrance to the school from the Square. There was a stream of strangers coming on campus. My father walked home shortly after sunset. There had already been conflicts between marshals and students. When he [Dr. Talbert] got home, his face was as ashen as it

31

had been after his first heart attack two years earlier. He let us know that he would have to go back on campus to supervise putting out an emergency edition of the Daily Mississippian urging calm, sadly too late. He asked me if I wanted to go with him.

We walked in silence along University Avenue. Both sides of the street were lined with parked cars as if for a football game. We could hear the sounds of crowd even before we saw the action centered on the Lyceum. As we approached Brady Hall we could see National Guard truck with its canvas on fire giving eerie lighting to the smoke of the tear gas and rioters' profiles. I remember the rifle fire, distinguishable from that of pistols—and the explosion of tear gas grenades, and the yells of the crowd. My father remained calm, and I wondered how this fit with his combat experience in the Pacific.

When we got into Brady Hall, the interior seemed eerily quiet, though busy and certainly business-like. My father was calm and intense as he began putting a special issue together. I have no idea how long we were there. As a high school senior with no role more than a witness to history I felt useless, only catching glimpses of my father, his students, and the press room staff called in for this strange and unexpected duty. As I was to learn later as a professional journalist, this is standard operating procedure in crisis.

After the special edition went to press, we began the long walk home. Our car had been burned earlier in the afternoon while my father was attending conferences. We paused at the end of the walkway leading from Brady to University Avenue and looked back at the Lyceum. The strange sights and sounds of the rioting still haunt me today. I saw both sadness and anger in my father's face as we turned and walked home. I don't remember us saying a word in all that time.

After Meredith was registered for classes, the department soon resumed normal, less event-driven news education. Under Talbert, in addition to standard academic classes in a journalism curriculum, the department began adding extracurricular opportunities for students to apply their knowledge. There was of course the award-winning weekly student paper *The Mississippian*, which was a major training ground for editors and reporters of the future. In 1961 the student-produced *Mississippi Magazine* was started. In an early volume appeared the iconic photo essay of William Faulkner by student Ed Meek. These were some of the last photos made of Faulkner. The Mississippi Advertising Institute provided a training venue for students to actually develop advertising campaigns for businesses.

1971: *Daily Mississippian* reporters, Berkley Hudson, Ann Leftwich, Steve Bailey and Lester McAlister.

A major component of the department's activities involved multiple workshops and clinics for high school newspaper and yearbook editors and their advisors. The Mississippi Press Institute, initially a two-day affair [*see appended interview with Fran Talbert*] grew to be a week-long summer training session on campus. The institute included assisting in the publication of *The Mississippian* and was the first contact many future journalism students had with the department. Talbert felt that it was as important for him to recruit for top-notch students as it was for a football coach to seek the best players in high school.

Talbert asked a lot of his students, pushed them to obtain summer jobs on newspapers, and used his extensive contacts with editors and publishers to make jobs and internships available. This professional experience, growing out of well-taught courses in journalism, made Ole Miss a fertile hunting ground for prospective employers. In his annual report for the 1956-57 academic year, Talbert boasted that 20 jobs were available for every Ole Miss journalism graduate.[35]

As the department developed, Talbert began the initial process of seeking accreditation, hoping to gain national recognition. In 1958 he wrote the central administration at Ole Miss:

A major immediate goal is to attain accreditation for the Department of Journalism by the American Council on Education for Journalism. It is the long-range goal of the Department to help build in Mississippi a sounder newspaper industry and a finer journalistic leadership through instruction, research and service.[36]

Any attempt at national accreditation that the department was working toward had to be put on hold in the wake of the struggles the entire university underwent in the aftermath of the Meredith riot. It took a future chairmanship under Ron Farrar for that landmark advancement to come to fruition.

BACK IN HARNESS—Dr. Sam S. Talbert, chairman of the Department of Journalism at the University of Mississippi, was surprised by his journalism students with a giant "Happy Birthday" sign this week on the eve of his return to work after a two-months illness. The sign was strung from two trees across the entrance to the journalism building on the Ole Miss campus.

Talbert's enthusiasm was infectious. Students and faculty colleagues loved Dr. Sam and patiently tolerated his occasional temper tantrums. Donna Hobson ('68), later to become a newspaper editor, recalls:

> There are so many stories about Dr. Sam that I could tell.... His chair squeaked to the point that it was very annoying, so my fellow student worker and I decided to take it to the back shop of the *Daily Mississippian* for oil. We took the chair back to the office and thought all was well until he walked down the hall and followed the trail of oil that we had left behind. We heard words that we had never heard before. Also at that time parking behind the j-building was restricted to faculty and staff, so as juniors we weren't allowed to utilize the lot. When we asked Dr. Sam what we could do he muttered an expletive and said we should just write a letter for staff parking permits, since we could sign his name better than he could. Then there was the time one of my fellow students who was enrolled in photography developed the paper instead of the film. I don't think Dr. Sam ever recovered!

Dr. Sam's eruptions were short lived and delivered without rancor. But they could be memorable. Barbara Shackelford ('71), recalls a couple of them:

> One summer I helped Dr. Sam with one of the yearbook conferences held each year. For some reason, this class was made up primarily of nuns. One particular day he made them an assignment—I don't remember what it was—and the next day when they turned their work in, he slammed it down on his desk and declared that they had violated every (I'll let you fill in the expletive) rule he tried to teach them! I wanted to crawl under the table! One afternoon I came to work and Dr. Sam was reared back in his chair with his feet on the desk. I asked if he had anything special for me to do that day. He very emphatically said, "Yes, you can help me find my damned glasses." They were on his head, as they often were.[37]

"I loved him dearly," Shackelford adds. "His great gift to students was to make them believe they could do anything."

Talbert continued and added to programs begun by Forbes during the department's infancy—the Mississippi Scholastic Press Association, the Editor's Short Course and the deep, invaluable ties with the Mississippi press.

1968: First staff to be called the *Daily Mississippian* staff, though *The Mississippian* had gone daily in 1962. L-r: Joe Lee, George Fair, Richard Smathers, Jennifer Bryon, Betty Carlisle, Micke Crosby, Charles Overby, Johnny Johnson, Tonto Tallie, Mike Larroux, Clant Seay, Bobo Champion, Vanci Campbell, Roger Cox and Steve Guyton.

From the beginning of his tenure as chairman of the Ole Miss Deapartment of Journalism Talbert recruited female students and helped break the gender barrier at a time when reporting, especially crime reporting and investigation of corrupt law enforcement and political scandal, was considered a man's job. Many of Talbert's female students went on to distinguished careers in journalism. Among them were Florence King, Sidna Brower, Mary-Lynn Kotz, Nancy Mason, Bettye Simmons, Kathrine Webb, Lee Cox, and Julie Smith. Several dedicated books to Talbert.

Nancy Mason, now assistant professor of Spanish at Dalton State College, recalls, "When I give presentations on my early days as a writer/journalism student, I like to mention how Dr. Sam called my bluff after my freshman year when I said I wanted to work that summer on a "big city" newspaper. He helped me get a job as chief of *The Commercial Appeal*/Helena, Ark, Bureau." She remembers that the door to the Talberts' home was always open and she felt welcome to drop in at all hours to talk to him or Mrs. Talbert:

> When we went off on summer job adventures, Dr. Sam kept in touch with long, rambling chatty letters filled with student and college gossip so we could stay in touch and not

36

lose our connection. He had confidence in us but never did I feel that he was "throwing us under the bus" with sometimes overwhelming challenges. His mantra always was "start at the top, then work down," and never settle for a place at the bottom to start with. He could be brutally honest and never minced words when he expressed an opinion, but I always knew that he cared about the journalism students and had a gift for getting the most out of us. His encouragement and confidence in us is what makes that connection so vibrant even after half a century.[38]

In 1958, Talbert and Ole Miss Chancellor John D. Williams created an award that would become nationally known and respected. Called "The Silver Em," the award would go annually to honor a distinguished journalist with a Mississippi background. The first recipient was George W. Healy, an Ole Miss graduate who had won accolades for his editorship of the *Times-Picayune*. In future years the Silver Em awardees would amount to, in effect, a Hall of Fame for journalists who were born in, or worked in, Mississippi.[39]

Hall of Fame member Charles Overby, for whom the Overby Center is named, was DM editor-in-chief in 1968.

Journalism students at Ole Miss became part of Dr. Sam's extended family. Dr. Sam and his wife invited students to their home on frequent occasions. The students enjoyed being around the Talbert's seven children, a son and six daughters. Dr. Sam did some amateur painting and sketching. But perhaps the most interesting painting was done by the Talbert children. Dr. Hoar recalls:

> On a large canvas, or piece of beaverboard, he (Talbert) had each of his children paint part of a story—any story, anything they wanted to say or paint or draw. The result was absolutely charming. Somehow those children, all girls but one, and of all ages from advanced teens to one not more than four or five, .. .contributed to a family story.[40]

Dr. Sam's creativity took many forms. One of these, begun while he was an undergraduate at the University of Florida, was whittling, which later evolved into a form of woodcarving. "One day I was just playing around with an interesting looking limb and made a figure from it," he said. "The dean of the School of Architecture at the University of Florida saw some of my work and bought it for quite a bit more than I thought it was worth. From then on, every time I ran short on money I would carve a few figures and sell them."[41]

Sam and Fran Talbert

Talbert's wife Frances Eleanor Selzer Talbert was, in her own way, as lively and accomplished as her husband. Born in Independence, Iowa, she, too, had served in World War II, as a Lieutenant in the Women's Army Air Force. She met Sam in Atlantic City in 1943, and they were married soon after Talbert returned from the Pacific in November 1944. Mrs. Talbert, who put her active career on hold to raise their seven children, remained a registered dietitian and was a founding member of the Mississippi Dietetics Association. After Dr. Talbert's death, she resumed her career and became the founding dietitian with the North Mississippi Regional Center. She was very active in Oxford's St. John's Catholic Church. When she died, at 96 in 2010, she was the church's longest serving parishioner.[42] Beyond all this, she found the time and the energy to entertain Ole Miss journalism students at any number of departmental parties. Indeed, all of Dr. Sam's students who had accepted any of his open invitations had been in the Talbert home at one time, or more, during their undergraduate years.

In 1970 Talbert went on a statewide speaking tour on behalf of the Ole Miss Department of Journalism. His message was the impact of mass media and information overload, which he compared to hypertrophy. Simple, direct communication along with intelligent interpretation of the facts, he told his audiences, was the role of the modern journalist. "The reporter who relates incidents but does not consider consequences stirs a witch's brew." He felt that the press had let the public down by failing to interpret contemporary events, and that journalists had a responsibility to tell the truth about potentially violent issues. "We are a state of people, black and white, which believes in the Bible," he said. "We do not have to go beyond that book to find the truths which pierce the hypertrophy of communications."

Talbert's concerns for his students did not end when they were graduated. Jesse Phillips, publisher of the then-weekly *Oxford Eagle*, provides a more or less typical example. He recalls:

> ... very vividly asking Dr. Sam for lunch and a counseling period. At this
> time, we were considering the conversion from letterpress reproduction to the offset process. Along with this was the idea of a central printing plant whereby other papers from surrounding towns might be printed. Dr. Sam expressed a positive attitude about both...and within a year both were accomplished.
>
> During this same "sitting" we discussed the feasibility of taking the big step to a daily operation. Again, Dr. Sam said, "We've got a growing community and I think the time is very near when you should change to a daily operation. You should not wait."
>
> This advice was kindly, like a father telling a baby to jump into his arms from a great height. It took a good bit of faith for us, but we did and now feel it was the right thing, beyond any doubt.
>
> The fine experience of a "father to son" type of relationship that Dr. Sam and this writer enjoyed can be multiplied hundreds of times with other students of his....[43]

THE UNIVERSITY OF MISSISSIPPI
UNIVERSITY, MISSISSIPPI

May 24, 1971

Dear Jesse and Nina,

Now that your new baby, the daily OXFORD EAGLE, seems to be home healthy and howling, I feel that I can offer my congratulations without fear of having to dodge a flying typewriter.

Frankly, I didn't expect the baby to be so big or so healthy at birth. When we were talking about prospects a couple of years ago, I even said it would be easier to produce a daily than a great big weekly. You all probably have been thinking that I am the biggest liar or ignoramous in Mississippi. But just wait until things get "organized" and you'll see.

It was getting a little boring every year at the Mississippi Press Convention to call out, for first place in general excellence among weeklies: "THE OXFORD EAGLE." Darned if it doesn't seem that we will have to go on with the same routine, with THE OXFORD EAGLE still winning first place among dailies in its division--with Nina sitting snugly in the audience waiting for the inevitable top award.

Oxford has a right to be proud of its new daily and the people who are doing so much work to make it good. But more than pride is involved. We will see soon that the commerce and general welfare of the community will be greatly served by your courageous step forward.

Sam S. Talbert
Chairman, Dept. of Journalism
University

A department chairmanship is a year-round job. Even when not teaching in summer school, he usually came in almost every day during the summer to take care of the mail and other business.

He never forgot the importance of practical experience, even for professors. In 1960 he took a sabbatical to work as a copy editor on the Memphis *Commercial Appeal*. During his time there he suffered his first heart attack. It was severe, and was followed by several others during the years that followed. After recovery from that first heart attack he wrote Frank Ahlgren, editor of *The Commercial Appeal*, "I am really amazed to find out how much more stimulating and effective my classes have become as a result of my work on *The Commercial Appeal*, adding, "I think someone should pass a law requiring every college professor—in any field—to work . . . on a large newspaper."

He rallied after each cardiac setback and resumed his duties. He also continued to write his weekly "Local Business" column carried by dozens of newspapers.

In 1972, The Mississippi Scholastic Press Association voted to create a special award for Dr. Sam. It was the first-ever "Golden Em," to be presented at the same ceremony as the Silver Em. But on April 25, 1972, less than two weeks before the ceremony, Dr. Sam died. He was 54.

Tributes and expressions of grief and sympathy poured in from throughout the nation. Nina Goolsby, editor of *The Oxford Eagle*, spoke for many when she wrote:

> Dr. Talbert has been a great inspiration to us.... Journalism students at Ole Miss found more than just a teacher or a department head. They found a friend... who was always interested in their welfare and in seeing they gave their very best. It was a delight to have Dr. Talbert drop into our office.... Through the years the life of this man has affected more newspaper people in the State of Mississippi than any one man I have ever known, and we will always remember.[44]

POSTHUMOUS MEMORIALS FOR SAM TALBERT

In the months, years and even decades after his death, colleagues and former students set up permanent memorials to Dr. Talbert, many designed to continue the development of the profession he loved.

First, during the Mississippi Scholastic Press Association (MSPA) high school Press Institute the spring following his death, Dr. Talbert was posthumously awarded the first Gold Em Award. The award was accepted on behalf of the Talbert family by William B. Street, political columnist of *The Commercial Appeal*.

In May 1972, the Mississippi state Senate passed Resolution No. 576 commending the "life and works of Dr. Samuel S. Talbert and recognize(d) the large gap in the ranks of educators and journalists left by his passing." This resolution was closely followed in June by a resolution by the general faculty of the University of Mississippi in recognition of Dr. Talbert's many contributions to the school.

In 1974 the Mississippi Press Association set up the Samuel Stubbs Talbert Research Fund in journalism as a non-profit foundation to finance research conducted by graduate students in journalism in the state. About this same time, the Department of Journalism established the Samuel Stubbs Talbert Lambda Sigma Award to be presented to the student contributing the most to community service through journalism. Sam's widow Fran Talbert presented the first award in 1974 to Otis Tims, then a senior and editor of the *Daily Mississippian*.

In 1986, the Mississippi Press Association created the Hall of Fame for Mississippi journalists, inducting Dr. Talbert among the initial ten honorees.

In 2004, Ellis Nassour, author and former *New York Times* and *Daily News* journalist who graduated from Ole Miss in 1961, donated his extensive media collection to the University of Mississippi Library. He named a portion of the collection after journalism chair Sam Talbert, citing him as one of the mentors who provided him inspiration.

In 2008, the Department of Journalism faculty at the University of Mississippi renamed the prestigious Silver Em to honor Dr. Talbert. The recipient that year of the newly renamed Samuel Talbert Silver Em Award was Ron Agnew, executive editor of the *Clarion-Ledger*. Then Department Chair Samir Husni said in an interview, "It was Samuel Talbert who started the Silver Em to recognize the great work of journalists either from Mississippi or who've made a significant contribution to the state. The faculty wanted to rename the award in honor of a person who met those same standards. No one fits that mold better than Samuel Talbert."

At the same time in 2008 during the rededication of the newly renovated Farley Hall, which was home to the Department of Journalism, one of the classrooms was named the Samuel S. Talbert Reading Room. The plaque in the room explains this honor: "During the tenure of Dr. Samuel S. Talbert as Chairman of the Department of Journalism from 1957 to 1972, the reading room displayed newspapers from around Mississippi and the nation, served as a classroom and as a special place for faculty-student interaction. The Reading Room, endowed by Ed Meek, honors 'Dr. Sam' for his love of and devotion to students, and honors his wife, Fran, who welcomed students into their home like members of an extended family."

Jere Hoar

The Professor, the Author

1974: Jere R. Hoar, outstanding teacher.

There may be some truth in that ancient, cruel observation about professors: "Those who can, do. Those who cannot, teach." Fact is, a fair number of professors are pretty good at both. But not many have succeeded in either endeavor as brilliantly as Dr. Jere Hoar, whose teaching career was woven deep into the fabric of the journalism program at Ole Miss throughout most of its history. And whose career as an author has won him a national audience as well as great respect within the literary community — all the more remarkable because he only began writing fiction in earnest after he reached the age when most folks retire. His first novel was published when he was 73. Unusual, but not necessarily surprising to anyone familiar with the intelligent, resolute, complex personality that is Dr. Jere Hoar.

Within weeks of deciding to remain at Ole Miss and take over as chair of the fledgling program in journalism, Samuel Talbert hired Jere Hoar, an energetic young man, already well-known to him and whose credentials were impressive.

He already had solid experience with newspapers; Jere's father had been a publisher and early on he involved his son in the family business. "I felt the rumble of newspaper presses through the soles of my shoes when I was a boy," he recalls.[45] Later, he was a reporter or news editor for two weekly newspapers and a small daily, editor of a trade publication and a magazine freelancer. When he volunteered during the Korean War, he served most of his hitch as an Air Force journalist. He had paid his professional dues.

And he had sturdy academic tickets as well: A bachelor's degree from Auburn, a master's from Ole Miss, and completion of course work and comprehensive examinations for a doctorate in mass communications from the University of Iowa — the oldest doctoral program in the field and one which carried considerable prestige throughout the academy.

None of this came easily.

1976 *Daily Mississippian*: Peggy Booth, news editor; Karen Heern, managing editor.

Jere Richmond Hoar was born in Dyersburg, Tennessee, in 1929, just as the nation was plunging into its deepest economic depression. Jere's father necessarily shifted from one job to another, serving at various times as a lieutenant and trouble-shooter in the Civilian Conservation Corps, a quasi-military program designed to provide manual labor for conserving natural resources and financial support for the families of unemployed young men.[46] The Hoar family was on the move more or less continually, and by the time Jere Hoar was ready to enter college he had attended 13 separate elementary and high schools, ranging from Utah and California to South Carolina and Alabama, with stops in between.

The day after the Japanese bombed Pearl Harbor, Eldon Hoar volunteered for overseas duty. He served with distinction in the Pacific and rose to the rank of colonel. After the war Col. Hoar bought the *Troy Messenger*, a small daily in Alabama. He later became editor and publisher of *The Oxford Eagle*.

Somewhere along the line, Jere Hoar developed a desire to become a teacher. "Desire" may not be the right term. To him, it must have been more like a calling. And few ever treated a calling with more respect, or labored harder to answer it.

A first step was to earn a master's degree. He chose Ole Miss. His family had by now moved to Oxford. Gerald Forbes ambitiously listed a master's among the journalism department's offerings, although it had never awarded one. Hoar was offered a $1,400 instructor's fellowship by the School of Business, following a recommendation by Forbes, but he declined the offer. It would have required half time teaching and half time graduate classes, doubling the time he'd spend earning a master's.

Jere Hoar and friend

The Department offered too few graduate courses to meet his needs so he was permitted to take two courses in playwriting (one taught by a renowned visiting playwright), and two courses in English, "The Great Critics" taught by the university's austere Shakespearian scholar, and one in Emerson and Thoreau taught by Harry Modean Campbell, a Fugitive.[47] The excitement of delving into ideas from different disciplines at the graduate level affirmed his plans for a career in the academy, and he was wise enough to know that a doctorate would solidify his credentials. The University of Iowa's doctoral program was selective, nationally respected, and was multi-disciplinary as well. He was not only accepted there but was awarded an assistantship.

A Ph.D. in mass communications from Iowa would lead to offers from many institutions. But Ole Miss was Jere's favorite, so much so that when a vacancy opened up there he was willing to accept it, even though his doctoral dissertation was yet to be written. Dr. Sam Talbert was eager to hire the young scholar. He wrote an offer letter on April 1, 1956, but included a strong cautionary note:

"There are too many Ph.D.s without dissertations floating around. I think there are many reasons why you should stay (at Iowa) until you complete the degree. A change in atmosphere and routine can be ruinous at the point you have reached…. It seems like a simple matter to take a full-time job and finish the dissertation at night. It's not, brother -- particularly when you have removed yourself from fellow sufferers. It means putting off until tomorrow until tomorrow becomes years and perhaps forever. Don't let me or anyone else tempt you right now.[48]

But on April 29 he offered different advice: "I understand that you may not finish your degree this summer—and I remember expressing very strong advice that you stay at UI until everything is completed. Now that my own interests are involved, I retract the advice and hope that you will consider finishing your work in the future."[49]

If Dr. Sam held the job open for Hoar until he had the degree in hand, it would be a gamble, since other universities — better paying ones, offering less demanding teaching assignments — would be making offers. And Dr. Sam knew Jere Hoar. Talbert liked to hire people he knew personally and had taught. He knew the younger man's fondness for Oxford and Ole Miss. There is no evidence that he even considered another person for the job.

But what was the significance of the phrase "Now that my own interests are involved" in his offer letter of May 8? That morning Talbert had made his own final decision to stay at Ole Miss.[50] Two days later he made another pitch: "I consulted professor Moeller (director of the mass communications program at Iowa) and he said he "does not think you would be unwise to come to Mississippi."[51] Talbert went on to describe the low pressure situation in the Mississippi department, and the ample time that would be left over after teaching. He suggested that a new assistant professor (Hoar had never taught before) would find time after preparing eight new courses the first year to complete the dissertation without undue delay.[52]

This was probably not disingenuous, although it sounds so. Colleagues recalled that Talbert rarely, or never, found it necessary to prepare for class. He was ready to discuss almost any subject at length.[53]

Feeling that professor Moeller's statement that Jere Hoar "would not be unwise" to take the Mississippi job lacked enthusiasm, two days later Talbert added another recommendation. He wrote, our Provost at Ole Miss, Dr. Alton Bryant, "is very pleased at the possibility of employing you for the vacancy."

Since then Hoar had completed course work and comprehensive examinations for a Ph.D. degree in mass communications at the University of Iowa. If Talbert hired Hoar, he would have a generalist to teach a variety of courses. A small department needed generalists, Talbert was convinced. Not only that, but Talbert saw a competitive advantage in having two Ph.D.s in the teaching field. There were few doctorates of any kind held by journalism faculty members in southern colleges and universities. Almost all of those were in the field of Education.

In his first offer letter to Hoar, Talbert wrote:

> There is no question about the job here being open to you if you want it —at least as far as I am concerned.... I know that you will get better monetary offers elsewhere, but I believe you will get some extra compensations from the work here. You know of course what most of them are. However, I think we have an informality and lack of pressure here that possibly won't be found elsewhere. I really don't think you will find a better situation anywhere....

In a series of letters of gentle persuasion—some mailed every two days—Talbert completed the sale. Talbert and Hoar each would teach 12 hours per semester. The chairman said his colleague could teach anything on the schedule he wanted so long as each course was different. It "didn't matter much" to Talbert what he, himself, taught. Talbert did "like to mix it up on similar courses so students will get some variety of viewpoint." In the first two semesters he suggested Hoar teach eight different courses: beginning editing, press photography, weekly newspaper management, feature writing, second semester reporting, law of the press, history of journalism and public opinion.

Hoar would earn $4,500 for nine months, without any promise of summer teaching. It was considerably less than was accepted by any of his Iowa cohorts finishing their doctorates. Talbert, as department chairman, was paid $5,800 at the time. That consumed most of the departmental budget. The only remaining items were $280 in wages (part-time secretarial and teaching help), $588.27 for supplies and expenses and $36.73 for equipment.

Shortly after his newly appointed assistant professor of journalism arrived on campus, Talbert said in the most casual way that Hoar would eventually teach each journalism course in the catalog. "I was accustomed to working hard, and so ignorant of the work loads expected of beginning professors I nodded agreement. Or, understanding of what faced me. There would be no time to work on my dissertation."

Because of his informal and casual approach to teaching, Talbert probably did not realize Hoar would spend hours in study and preparation for each class.

Though the journalism department was small, woefully understaffed and underfunded, Jere Hoar had accepted the job and all the advantages and disadvantages that went with it. Sentiment may have played a role in his decision. But one suspects he knew Ole Miss needed what he had to offer.

And that was considerable. In the years to come he would carry a heavy and varied teaching load—some 22 separate courses in his career, ranging from reporting at the beginning level to graduate seminars in Human Communications Theory. He would do his share of the kind of publishing that counts in academia, including refereed articles in the leading journals of four disciplines.[54]

Tall and slender and with something of a military presence, he was rather formal, especially in the classroom. If the teaching style of his mentor, Sam Talbert, and his later colleague, Gale Denley, was relaxed and good humored, the classes of Jere Hoar were serious business. He drove his students hard, and drove himself even harder.

And yet his greatest intellectual challenge was still ahead—passing the Mississippi bar exam without having attended law school.

By 1965 Jere Hoar had made up his mind to study law. Although political issues at the University of Mississippi prevented his attending a school of law, he would not be stopped. A program called the Mississippi Preceptorship in Law was an alternate route to eligibility to take the state bar examination. The lawyers in the respected Oxford firm, Freeland & Gafford, agreed to become Hoar's preceptors.

He began by taking a year's leave of absence from Ole Miss. Afterward he spent every minute he honorably could—summers, weekends, nights studying law and meeting the clerking requirements of the preceptorship.[55]

Some 338 persons had entered a preceptorship when Jere Hoar passed the bar exam in 1971, becoming the fifth such student to have done so. When the preceptorship program ended 13 years later, after 20 years of existence, with an unknown number of participants, 16 had passed the bar.[56]

But Hoar's objective had not been primarily to practice. He already had a Ph.D. and was senior professor in his department. The preceptorship provided a structure to delve into the law and learn more about it. That had been a goal since boyhood. The license to practice was a personal marker along the way to broadening his competence to teach.

His Communications Law course became the talk of the Ole Miss campus: It was, arguably, the most respected/dreaded class at the university.

"I remember it like it was yesterday," writes Rex Baker ('83). "'Mr. Baker, you just went down in flames.' If you didn't go down in flames at least once in Dr. Jere Hoar's Communications Law class, you weren't really a journalism major. A couple of weeks after I went down in flames, Dr. Hoar called on another student. He went down in flames. Dr. Hoar then asked me the same question. I timidly answered, to which Dr. Hoar replied 'Mr. Baker, that is correct.' I felt like I'd just been admitted to Harvard. I'm more proud of the B that I got in Communications Law than any other grade I ever received."[57]

Tom Bearden, ('71), later a television reporter and anchor, calls "Dr. Hoar the toughest teacher I ever had. He was direct, he demanded performance, and he was fair. Those are virtues that should be the foundation of any journalist's career. And his course on libel and slander law has kept me from ever being sued."[58]

Though it was designed for undergraduates in journalism, Hoar's Communications Law course attained such respect across the campus that it was cross-listed by the School of Law. And while Law School students could get full credit for completing the course, not many did.

Requirements for graduate journalism students and law students included a research paper.FN "On the first day of class there were a few law students present," recalls Robert Harter ('79). "By the second or third session, all of the law students had disappeared, for some strange reason. That class turned out to be the most demanding of any I have ever taken.... It also turned out to be one of my favorites."[59]

It was a favorite, too, of Gregory Lisby, Ph.D., J.D., who earned his M.A. degree at Ole Miss. He dedicated his book, *Mass Communication Law in Georgia*, to Dr. Jere Hoar, "a former professor who first helped combine my commitment to journalism with my love of the law." He inscribed a copy to "my first and best law professor. With gratitude..."

Tough as the Law course was, many students found other of Jere Hoar's classes equally challenging. Such as Gigi McMurray ('88), who later taught nursing at Vanderbilt and spent four years as a missionary in Honduras. She very nearly lost her religion over one journalism class. "Dr. Jere Hoar taught possibly the most dreaded and dreadful course at the university when I attended," she writes. "The course was entitled Public Opinion, and Public Opinion struck fear in every student.... I have only burned one notebook. It saddens me deeply today that I do not have that notebook. I go back to the principles I learned in that course possibly more than any other. As I ponder how the news is delivered in this country, especially after living outside it for four years, I am struck by many factors Dr. Hoar taught me.... Dr. Hoar not only prepared me to be a journalist, he prepared me to be an adult in this world who can filter all that I hear and see and read.... I am indebted to him."[60]

Hoar's Feature Writing course, which obviously required a different teaching method, was equally difficult. Early in the term, he would ask the class to set a goal for itself, the number of features the class could produce—and sell. The class members, usually juniors or seniors, would develop feature ideas and submit articles they thought were finished—usually to find Dr. Hoar, having spent considerable time evaluating each manuscript, give back the work for more and more polishing. That done, the piece was pronounced ready to send off, mostly likely to be accepted and published by a professional newspaper or magazine. In one more or less typical semester, his Feature Writing class of 25 sold about 100 articles. Few professors anywhere could drive their students and themselves to that kind of success.

1973 *Daily Mississippian*: Cris Fletcher, staff writer, photographer; Pepper Watson (seated), sports writer; Janice Guyton, features editor; Susan Nolan, staff writer; Cindy Dixon, women's editor.

Hoar labored for hours over graduate student seminar papers and theses when he was director of the department's small, but high quality, graduate program. Six of these MA recipients later earned doctorates in various fields, and went on to teach in universities.

When time permitted he would take on extra responsibilities, such as working with a student on an Independent Study basis. One such student, Steve Bailey ('72), writes "I also did a special tutorial with him (Dr. Hoar) on H. L. Mencken, which was my most satisfying experience at Ole Miss."[61]

Rudy Abramson, ('68), who became one of the country's leading reporters, operating primarily from the Washington bureau of the *Los Angeles Times*, inscribed one of his books: "For Jere Hoar, the great teacher, who helped generations of young people find their way—among them a young man from Arkansas who still treasures the friendship begun in Journalism 101."[62]

Jere Hoar's steely determination ruffled some feathers among students and faculty colleagues, but his teaching success was undeniable. Thus in 1974 his department chairman nominated him for an honor highly coveted at Ole Miss, the Outstanding Teacher Award. In part, the chairman's letter put it this way:

> In my years around a university, I have come to judge professors by one simple measure: Not by their personal following, not by classroom theatrics, not by anything except the quantity and quality of work they get from their students. Students work for Jere Hoar; many of them work through gritted teeth, no doubt, but they work nevertheless. Jere Hoar's Communications Law course, his Feature Writing course, his Communication Theory seminars are the best I have seen, and I know from personal experience how these same subjects are handled at Iowa, Missouri, Indiana and Southern Methodist University, to name four other fine institutions where I have either studied or taught. Indeed, Jere's Communication Theory seminar, which we teach at the master's level, would be a credit to any doctoral program in the field in America.
>
> ... I assume this award is not a contest of personal popularity. Jere Hoar is not universally popular; consciences rarely are. Yet a surprising number of students do feel close to him, simply because they understand he respects and likes his students too much to let them get away with anything but their best. Yet even those who don't like Jere Hoar now—or think they don't, anyway—usually become his greatest boosters in later years. Any number of journalism alumni have told me this. Perhaps the most graphic of them is a prominent White House correspondent, an Ole Miss graduate with whom I had dinner in Washington recently. Let me quote him directly: "When I was at Ole Miss I stayed mad at Jere Hoar," he said. "I thought he was a son-of-a-bitch. Now I realize he was the best teacher I ever had."[63]

Many other nominations for Jere Hoar were received by the selection committee, and he was presented the Outstanding Teacher Award that year, 1974. For one so dedicated to teaching, few honors on the planet would have meant more to him.

There would be other career honors, notably the Silver Em as he neared retirement. He served occasionally as a panelist for Mississippi Judicial College programs, and he was appointed a founding member of the governing committee of the American Bar Association Forum on Communications Law.

"My teaching strategy is simple," he wrote, in response to a request: "To lead (or push) the student as far as he can go, and then show him how he can go one step farther. A teacher of my type doesn't expect undergraduate popularity. He asks more than the student wants to give. There may be temporary resentment. Rewards come, if they do, in later years in letters, visits and lifelong friendships."[64]

Grateful former students honored his retirement by establishing a scholarship fund, well over $50,000, in his name. The scholarship, offering opportunity for journalism students far into the future, and the outstanding teacher award—recognition of Jere Hoar's extraordinary efforts for his students in the past—were a nice rounding of the career of a teacher who always gave his best, and encouraged and pushed students to achieve more than they thought they were capable of.

In 1986, after completing 30 years with the Department of Journalism at Ole Miss, he retired from full-time membership on the faculty. And though he continued to teach, on a part-time basis for six more years, he now had the freedom to pursue much more intensively what had been a lifelong dream, that is, to write fiction.

Jere Hoar's literary work came slowly—write, rewrite, polish. In his 60s he took classes under the celebrated short story writer Barry Hannah. "I'm working on one manuscript that is now old enough to vote," he wrote to a friend.[65] He wrote short stories at first, some 30 of them, and these were published in as many as 20 different literary journals. They were favorably reviewed, and some won awards.

Then he was stricken with a brutal case of Rocky Mountain Spotted Fever, a disease which incapacitated him for months. During that time he dug up some old, unpublished short story manuscripts and submitted them because, as he told Robert L. Hall, "I didn't have enough energy to write new ones."[66] Some of the short stories were begun as chapters in an unpublished novel, *Levitation*. Eventually he had accumulated enough short stories, more than enough, for a book. This collection became *Body Parts*, published in 1997 by the University Press of Mississippi. It was the only university press-published fiction selected for inclusion in the New York Times list of the hundred best books of the year. Booklist evaluated it as one of the few books reviewed in the year "worthy of being chosen best book of the year."

Body Parts drew excellent reviews in leading national publications.

55

The critic from New York's *Newsday*, said, "It can pop chill bumps on your neck."[67] Such enthusiastic acceptance prompted inquiries from journalists into Jere Hoar's writing style. In one such interview, he explained:

Some writers find a method, style maybe, or a theme they like, and their stories thereafter show similarity. I'm not interested in doing that. Everything I've written has been different because the challenge is to learn craft and grow through work. If I can give you an example: A craftsman in wood may learn to make a handsome and useful Chippendale chair. A demand develops, or he enjoys making Chippendale chairs, or he feels compelled to make Chippendale chairs to meet market requirements, so he specializes in them. If I were a craftsman in wood, that would bore me. I'd like to make a Chippendale chair, then a Hepplewhite table and then an Empire sofa.[68]

Literary competition honors accumulated: One manuscript, "The Snopes Who Saved Huckaby," was a co-winner in 1994 of the Faulkner Society's William Faulkner Short Story Competition for Fiction. The judge was Allan Gurganus. Gordon Weaver chose "Dark Heart" winner of the Kansas Arts Council/Kansas Quarterly Award. There were others, among them Hoar's novel-length manuscript, *Levitation,* winner of the Southern Writer's Conference competition. The contest judge, Ernest Gaines, author of *The Autobiography of Miss Jane Pittman,* said of Hoar's *Levitation* manuscript, "You will never meet in all your life two greater con men than Jimmy Lake, an evangelist minister, and his associate, Mr. Gooch, the owner of a carny show and an ace at flying a hot-air balloon, especially when it is necessary to get out of town quickly."[69] *Levitation* never got published, however.

"I offered it to Elizabeth McKee, Flannery O'Connor's agent," Hoar recalls. "She accepted it and was so convinced of its worth she offered it at auction. What she got back instead of bids were compliments on the writing. The marketing people in seven top publishing houses apparently thought they couldn't sell *Levitation.* Having had that experience, I resolved that the ideas in my next novel would be wrapped in a compelling and exciting yarn."[70]

Which they were. But he saw no reason why good writing need be sacrificed. The novel he would write next was *The Hit.* It was, as one reviewer saw it, "Mississippi Noir, a gritty, steamy story that reminded some of the hard-hitting style of James M. Cain in *The Postman Always Rings Twice,* or Dashiel Hammett's *Maltese Falcon.*"

John Grisham, arguably the most successful novelist of the age, said, "*The Hit* is lean, fast, unpredictable and immensely enjoyable. When I finished I said, 'I wish I'd written that.'"[71] Notable literary figures joined in pre-publication praise—Jim Harrison, Tom McGuane, Barry Hannah, Julie Smith, and Steve Yarbrough.

The reviewer at *U.S.A. Today* wrote: "Reading *The Hit* is a lesson in great writing. The artistry of the prologue alone inspires awe." The reviewer for the *Atlanta Journal Constitution* noted that "crime fans will thoroughly enjoy the seamier qualities of noir well done, while high minded types will flip over Hoar's crystalline style." *PW Daily for Booksellers* called *The Hit* "a page-turning literary treasure."

In a time when book sections were disappearing, book pages shrinking, and book page editors were being reassigned, *The Hit* received 22 known reviews—all but one favorable.

The Hit firmly placed Jere Hoar in the front ranks of Southern authors, rich company, especially for a man who'd spent 36 years of his career as a university professor, known primarily for his success at teaching mass media law. But Dr. Hoar had also taught many hundreds of students better ways to write. In "retirement" he was no longer teaching writing, but demonstrating it. *The Hit* was republished as a trade paperback by New American Library, and published in France and Poland. It was a notable book of the year selection of the *Kansas City Star*, and was the Independent Publisher Association's choice as best mystery or thriller of the year.

In the autumn of 2010, Jere Hoar suffered a massive stroke. Buoyed by support and encouragement from family, fellow townspeople, former students and former colleagues, he began the long, arduous journey toward recovery. A few weeks later, his partial paralysis on the mend, he was able to resume some of his creative projects. He went back to his home just outside Oxford, on a small farm where his daughter and two sons had grown up; where he had trained English Setter bird dogs, raised Tennessee Walking Horses and learned to compete in herding trials with a talented Tervuren herding dog and a flock of St. Croix sheep. It is a lovely setting, a place where, slowly, with discipline and great precision, he would write some more.

S. Gale Denley

The Down Home Professional

S. Gale Denley, general manager, Student Media Center.

If Jere Hoar exemplified intellectual and academic excellence in Ole Miss journalism, S. Gale Denley was the point man for professionalism.

An easygoing, shambling presence, Gale Denley was first and foremost a journalist, a skilled newspaperman/professor whose students understood that he practiced what he taught. He was a third-generation community newspaper publisher; his grandfather had bought the *Coffeeville Courier* in 1910, and Gale and his father took over the *Calhoun County Journal* at Bruce in 1953. When Dr. Sam Talbert offered him a faculty position at Ole Miss, it was with the understanding that Gale could continue as publisher of the popular weekly at nearby Bruce. It proved to be an ideal match, one that would bring a much-needed additional dimension to the program.

Outside of his immediate family—his wife JoAnne and their offspring handled much of the work at the *Calhoun County Journal* while Gale was teaching—two things seemed to mean most to Gale Denley: Newspapers and Mississippi. Gale was able to combine his love for both during his long and distinguished career at Ole Miss.

He knew, and was known by, virtually every newspaper editor and publisher in the state. And respected by them, especially for his wit and for his knowledge of the complex machinery and processes used in the manufacture of newspapers. He possessed a keen, and up-to-the-minute, understanding of it all, from cameras to typesetting machines to presses and folders. In the midst of the industry's sweeping technological change, some Mississippi publishers refused to buy a new piece of equipment or adopt a new technology without first checking with Gale Denley. This popularity and respect did not inflate his ego. Students and faculty colleagues found him unpretentious and self-deprecating. So did fellow journalists. He was arguably the best-liked man in the state press association, which conventions he rarely missed. Later he became perhaps the only journalism professor in America ever elected president of his state press association.

Denley was never much impressed with the inner workings of the academy—especially the bureaucratic infighting that seems to be endemic to so many campuses. Indeed, he was fond of quoting a cynical comment famously attributed to Dr. Henry Kissinger: "The reason academic battles are so ferocious is because the stakes involved are so small."

Students, however, were a different matter, and Gale loved teaching them. His laid-back lecture style, much like that of Dr. Sam Talbert, did not follow the methodologies presumably prescribed by Colleges of Education, but he got his points across. And, in his own avuncular way, he shrewdly sized up which students had particular strengths and which did not.

In just one example, a Mississippi publisher phoned Denley about a journalism senior who had applied for a job with his paper. Denley acknowledged that the kid was a good sort, but then enumerated weaknesses that the publisher ought to know about. "Well," the publisher replied, stunned, "if you ever find one you do think *would* work for me, I hope you'll let me know." Denley's frank appraisals made professionals trust his judgment implicitly.

A second example: A journalism student desperately wanted to become editor of the *Daily Mississippian*. He never made it and was convinced that Prof. Denley, who was on the Publications Board, had prevented him getting the position. After the selection, the young man admitted that probably Denley had been right, sensing that he wasn't cut out for that job. Through his hurt, he increased his respect for Denley's judgment. Years later, he would write, he knew "as long as Gale Denley was at Ole Miss, the *Daily Mississippian* would do well. And, under his influence, the paper could survive a lot."[72]

While Denley refused to adopt the publish-or-perish mentality so sacred throughout the academy, he nevertheless was one of the most productive professors, in terms of research, on the University of Mississippi campus. Eschewing the scholarly, peer-reviewed journals which pave the academic road to promotions and tenure, Denley chose instead to write for his brothers and sisters in real-world journalism. He was the author of a nationally syndicated column on small business and advertising and later a statewide syndicated column on politics and general interests. His research articles were published in such professional journals as *Editor & Publisher*, *Publishers' Auxiliary*, *The Journalism Educator* and the *Bulletin of the American Society of Newspaper Editors*.

One of his research projects, a state-wide study of newspapers and political advertising, revealed that some publishers specifically raised their rates for political candidates, a practice that was not only unfair, but poor business. "It is my concern that if these frustrations are not resolved, and if understandable and equally equitable rate systems are not implemented, the high cost of getting elected may result in the sole use of the electronic media, on a public service basis, in election campaigns," Denley said. Reforms were subsequently enacted and new standards applied.[73] This study was one of many Denley produced. University deans and provosts may not have appreciated, or even comprehended, the value of such nuts-and-bolts research, but Denley's fellow journalists clearly did: In 2000 he was inducted into the Mississippi Press Association Hall of Fame.

Denley was particularly interested in scholastic journalism. For years he served as head of the Mississippi Scholastic Press Association. And he was a fierce protector of student press freedom. High School teachers who advised their student newspapers could be trapped in a vulnerable position, walking a tightrope between students who wanted to express their views and a principal who may consider press freedom injurious to the school's image. In those conflicts, the adviser could expect full and direct support from Prof. Denley at Ole Miss.

Beyond that, Denley made available a page each week in his *Calhoun County Journal* to the students of Bruce High School, who produced the articles and pictures and editorials. That page became their school newspaper. "I think printing the page is one of the better things we do," Denley said. "It's not unique to us but we've continued it when other papers have not."[74]

Apart from journalism, or perhaps entwined with it, Gale Denley loved Mississippi. He knew literally thousands of Mississippians and was on a first-name basis with governors and other top political leaders.

He seldom missed the prolonged, folksy and somewhat goofy annual event that is the Neshoba County Fair, where he would perch comfortably on a lawn chair alongside his closest friend, Sid Salter, "Perspective" editor of the Jackson *Clarion-Ledger,* and greet passers-by. On football Saturdays at Ole Miss, Denley could spend hours meandering through the tail-gate crowds that filled the Grove in front of the Lyceum—shaking hands, hugging and being hugged, accepting, or politely refusing, the numerous offers of food and drink from friends from all over the state. Few Mississippians were as popular. Or enjoyed their popularity more.

1977 *Daily Mississippian*: Laura Anderson, copy editor; Jimmye Sweat, news editor; Susie Payne, managing editor; Mike Austin, assistant editor; Dawn Ladner, news editor.

Because he was so versatile, Denley was thrust into a staggering variety of courses—reporting, editing, photojournalism, advertising, public relations, media management, supervision of school publications. His work with students, both in and out of class, made for some long days, and sometimes it was well into the evening before he could begin the 30-miles-or-so commute from Oxford to his home in Bruce. On one such evening, in 1989, Gale's car was struck on the driver's side by a pickup truck.

The damage was devastating.

"Gale sustained what I would call whole body trauma," recalled a close friend, teaching colleague and fellow newspaperman, Charles D. Mitchell.

"He bruised internal organs, broke lots of bones. Those who saw him in the hospital predicted he wouldn't survive."

He did survive, but the recovery was long and agonizing and incomplete. Denley increasingly used a cane in the years that followed.[75] Pain and all, Denley kept at it, mostly working as general manager of the million-dollar student media operation, until 1996, when he retired.

At his retirement reception, Denley characteristically deflected credit away from himself. "The main thing we've accomplished is the students and all that they have done, and that's the only yardstick that should be used in an educational institution.... The bottom line is to help the student who is here...."[76]

Denley firmly believed that journalism students learn through their own experience, and he tried to give people the freedom to do their jobs correctly.[77] Then, he added an understated, but pertinent footnote to his teaching philosophy: "Of course, students hear from me if they mess up."[78]

Retirement notwithstanding, the memories of Gale Denley's contributions to Ole Miss were not forgotten. In 2003, the university dedicated a shiny, state-of-the art student media center and named it in honor of S. Gale Denley.

The Center provides students a rich variety of media experiences, including:

- The *Daily Mississippian*, one of the largest, and highest regarded, campus newspapers in the nation.
- Rebel Radio 92.1, one of only a handful of student-run, yet commercially licensed, radio stations in the nation.
- News Watch, a live, half-hour television evening newscast.
- *The Ole Miss* yearbook

An incredible, multi-platform learning lab, a facility that journalism schools everywhere might envy, the S. Gale Denley Media Center is a fitting testament to the remarkable career of its namesake.

1977 *Daily Mississippian* staff: Mac DeMere and Mike Austin, reporters and Karen Crenshaw, local news editor.

Denley's health continued its painful decline after his retirement from Ole Miss. Complications from a kidney ailment worsened, and on August 28, 2008, he died. His funeral, at the Methodist Church in Bruce, brought together hundreds of friends and former students and fellow journalists from far and wide. One of the speakers was Charles Dunagin, widely respected former publisher of the McComb *Enterprise-Journal*: "Gale demonstrated an ability throughout his adult life to both practice and teach good journalism. Moreover, he thoroughly understood and appreciated Mississippi politics, history and the varied cultures that make up our rather complex society."

Charlie Mitchell, then editor of the *Vicksburg Post,* put it this way: "In the classroom and as a journalist, Gale Denley by talent and temperament influenced generations of journalists not to be afraid of anyone or anything but above all else to be fair."

Sid Salter of the Jackson *Clarion-Ledger* asserted that "Gale Denley was a gentle man who faced a lot of adversity in his life with courage and hope. Our friendship has been one of the great joys of my life...." He called Gale Denley "the most influential Mississippi journalism educator of his generation."[79] Hundreds of Denley's former students would agree.

Ronald T. Farrar

Accreditation

Dr. Ron Farrar, chair, Department of Journalism, 1973-1977.

When I was asked to write this history of journalism at Ole Miss, I stipulated that any discussion of my own experience should be handled by someone else. Other persons discussed in these pages have contributed far more than I to the development of the program. And others should be more objective in assessing my own relatively brief role in the story. However, it was later decided that a second author here would be, as they put it, awkward, and I was instructed to write my own chapter. What follows, then, is a collection of memories—good memories—about events that took place long ago.

Ole Miss in 1973 was one big family, and my wife Gayla and I immediately

65

fell in love with it. We identified with the area, the people and the almost lyrical atmosphere of Oxford and the university community.

Of even greater appeal to me, though, was the amazing—if not well known—quality of the journalism students and faculty and alumni of Ole Miss. The program's facilities and equipment were wretched, of course, but with luck these could be fixed. Good quality faculty and students are the keys, however, and Ole Miss had these already. The makings were there. The challenge would be to let the rest of the country know what kind of journalism graduates the University of Mississippi was producing. The road to that success ran through national accreditation. If attained, that stamp of accreditation meant that the graduates from Ole Miss would be placed on a par with those from Missouri, Northwestern, Stanford, anywhere.

My own introduction to journalism came at the University of Arkansas in the 1950s. I pledged a fraternity that doggedly pushed its freshmen to get involved in campus activities. I wandered into the office of the campus daily, the *Arkansas Traveler*, and got a job on the staff. Soon after, I attended a guest lecture by a great Mississippian, Hodding Carter, Sr., who had just published *Where Main Street Meets the River*, a book about his life with the *Delta Democrat-Times* of Greenville. I was captivated by his story of small-city journalism, and charged back into the *Arkansas Traveler* with renewed enthusiasm and eventually was elected editor of the paper. The *Traveler* we produced that year was, among much else, a priceless learning experience, and I've been hooked on journalism ever since.

After graduation I spent the summer on the *Arkansas Democrat*, a statewide daily published in Little Rock, before serving my hitch in the Army as an unremarkable second lieutenant. The week following my release from active duty I went to work on a small daily in Paragould, Arkansas and, six months later, I was hired by the *Arkansas Gazette*. The *Gazette* had just won two Pulitzers for its coverage of the desegregation crisis at Little Rock's Central High School. In this great newsroom I was surrounded by a wonderful mix of seasoned veterans and highly promising newcomers. It was a joy to work with them. But, after a couple of years, I found I had not lost the desire to run a newspaper. Also I knew I had a lot to learn, having never sold an ad or handled a production or circulation or accounting problem. When I mentioned this to some publisher friends, they invited me to take over as editor/manager of one of their three Northeast Arkansas weeklies, the *Trumann Democrat*.

That experience turned out well, happily. The paper prospered and gave me confidence that I had at least some promise as an editor/publisher. This was encouraging. Even better, while at Trumann, I met and married Gayla Dennis, who had just earned her master's degree at the University of Michigan and was teaching English at Arkansas State University in nearby Jonesboro. We decided that graduate school would help fill in some of the gaps in my professional background. I applied to several schools. Encouraging responses came back from Columbia and Stanford, but those institutions were well out of our price range. Eventually I enrolled at the University of Iowa, where I also got a job. It was as circulation manager of the *Daily Iowan*—a campus newspaper that was unusual in that it was home delivered to each student, no matter where he or she lived. (And some of them lived in strange places.) I had about fifty carrier boys, who faithfully got the paper delivered, even on frigid Iowa winter mornings. Unlike most campus papers, the *Daily Iowan* was a member of the Audit Bureau of Circulations, which strictly monitored subscriber service, and this required careful bookkeeping to assure advertisers precisely where their messages went. It wasn't the most glamorous job, but it, and the money Gayla earned as a clerk in the registrar's office, paid my way through the master's program.

As with most graduate students at Iowa, I got to do some teaching and discovered that I liked it. Liked it enough, in fact, to decide to shoot for a doctorate. This led me to the University of Missouri, not only a world-class journalism school, but one with a doctoral program geared to my interest in history. A former dean of the J-School was Dr. Frank Luther Mott, the only journalism professor who ever won a Pulitzer Prize in history. Long since retired, dean Mott still came on occasion to the office, and we talked a number of times. It was he, in fact, who suggested that for my dissertation I should write a biography of Charles G. Ross, a distinguished journalist who became press secretary and confidant to his boyhood friend, Harry S. Truman. Armed with a letter from dean Mott, I was given access to the Ross papers in the Truman Library at Independence, and the research not only resulted in a dissertation but the makings of a book.

These were not written at Missouri, though, but at Indiana University, where I had eagerly accepted the offer of a teaching position—and a paycheck. My course work was completed by now, and it would have been better, and certainly easier, to finish the dissertation before taking on a full-time job. But I had a wife and a baby and some debt to worry about. Indiana University turned out to be a welcoming place, a fine environment. My adjustment to teaching—rarely easy, especially while finishing a dissertation—was made more bearable by the presence of Dr. I. Wilmer Counts, a top-of-the-line photographer and faculty colleague with whom I had worked in Little Rock. Will Counts was a great teacher, much beloved by his students, and his family did much to help my family and me adapt to those impressive surroundings.

After six years at Indiana, I had been promoted to associate professor rank and recommended for tenure, but, somewhat rashly, I felt I could handle a department chairmanship. The only one open in 1970 was at Southern Methodist University in Dallas, a tiny, frail department with two faculty and 40 majors. But the 70s years were exciting times for journalists, what with Watergate and Woodward and Bernstein demonstrating the power of the press—and the department grew rapidly, soon with 200 majors and seven faculty. SMU was and is a fine private institution with excellent students, but expensive and with priorities in business, law and the sciences. Because of that, and because there were then 30 other journalism programs in Texas, I couldn't see an extended future in Dallas. When the chairmanship at Ole Miss became available, I decided to apply. This proved to be one of the best decisions I ever made.

12A—The Oxford Eagle—Thursday, November 7, 1974

Journalism memorial

Mrs. Samuel S. Talbert, widow of the long-time chairman of the University of Mississippi Department of Journalism, discusses with Dr. Ronald Farrar, current chairman, pledges supporting the newly established Samuel Stubbs Talbert Research Fund in Journalism at Ole Miss. The total now stands at $4,000.

Getting journalism at Ole Miss accredited meant dealing with some problems, not the least of which were campus facilities and politics. After World War II, Chancellor J. D. Williams had decided to start a journalism program, this largely in response to demands of returning veterans for programs that could help them get jobs. The faculty in liberal arts, the biggest and most powerful unit at Ole Miss, did not want journalism at all. Following that rejection by liberal arts, Chancellor Williams offered journalism to the School of Business, which accepted it. Journalism involves advertising, which is a part of commerce. (As would be reaffirmed years later, with journalism's highly successful Integrated Marketing Communications program.)

When Ole Miss Chancellor Porter Fortune got my request that our tiny Department of Journalism seek national accreditation in 1975, he approved it—knowing that this would be an expensive and risky undertaking, with embarrassing results if accreditation were denied. After the lengthy pre-visit self-study book had been completed, and before the team arrived for an on-site visit, I got a summons to meet with the Chancellor. He knew the visiting team would meet with him first, and that much stock would be placed in his opinion of the journalism unit. "Now, Ron," he said, "what do you want me to tell these people?" Hoping that he would ask, I had brought along a list of talking points. Evidently he used them all, and Porter Fortune was one hell of a salesman. The tone he set with the visiting team did us a world of good.

Even so, what followed wasn't easy or pleasant. When the team first set foot in Brady Hall, they paced slowly up and down the creaking corridors of that ancient frame house. When they stepped into my tiny office, the team leader's first words were, "Is this it?" He was from Los Angeles, an administrator at the University of Southern California. The second member was a professor at Northwestern, and the third was dean of the College of Journalism and Communications at the University of Florida. Not the most likeable trio, though in fairness they were tasked to take their duty seriously. They did. They grilled each faculty member at length, examined every piece of equipment we had, pored over our meager budget, then had hour-long sessions with two separate groups of students, probing for weaknesses and evaluating the skills and knowledge and morale of the students. It was stressful. At one point, Greg Brock, a talented senior, came into my office to say, "Dr. Farrar, we know how much crap you're having to take from these guys, and we want you to know we appreciate what you're doing on our behalf."

Greg's comment made it all worthwhile. On the third day the team wrote its report and, heaven help us, listed our every weakness—budget, teaching loads, wretched facilities and equipment, substandard equipment, you name it. But they concluded, perhaps grudgingly, with a recommendation that Ole Miss journalism receive full national accreditation. They realized that, in spite of everything, the faculty was academically and professionally competent, and the students who came out of Ole Miss with a journalism degree were as well prepared as those from anywhere else.

We did have wonderful students. Greg Brock, previously mentioned, would become a top editor at the *New York Times*. Dan Goodgame would win a coveted Rhodes scholarship to Oxford and an editorship at *Time* magazine after that. Stephanie Saul, also at the *New York Times*, would be awarded a Pulitzer Prize, and Dennis Moore would be managing editor of *USA Today*. I can't remember them all, but they were a remarkable group. And they were well taught.

1977 *Daily Mississippian*: Laura Anderson, copy editor; Jimmye Sweat, news editor; Susie Payne, managing editor; Mike Austin, assistant editor; Dawn Ladner, news editor.

Jere Hoar was known to be the baddest, toughest professor at Ole Miss, certainly the most demanding, and the entire campus knew of his work and respected it. Gale Denley, who published a weekly newspaper at nearby Bruce as well as teaching a heavy class load, was known and admired throughout Mississippi journalism. Offset lithography was revolutionizing the newspaper industry at that time, and publishers in the region looked to Gale Denley for advice on new equipment purchases. Ed Meek, who headed the university's public information department, was revered in his additional part-time duty as a public relations professor. Beyond that, Ed and Gale introduced me to editors and publishers and broadcasters, most of them their personal friends, across the state. After my first year, we hired young Will Norton. All in all, I was there at a very good time.

Later we also hired R. Dean Mills, who had been the Moscow correspondent for the *Baltimore Sun*. A mutual friend, a professor at Iowa, mentioned to me that Dean had developed an interest in teaching. We had an opening just then, so I invited him to visit Ole Miss. He did, and was hired immediately. A remarkably bright and energetic fellow, Dean found that he enjoyed teaching, and knew his career prospects would be better if he had a doctorate. He enrolled at Illinois, earned his Ph.D. and rose rapidly within the academy. In 1989 he would become dean of the famous Missouri School of Journalism, a post he would hold with distinction for more than 25 years. While at Ole Miss, he made our already strong teaching staff stronger.

Accreditation brought us many benefits, one of them being an important transfer into the now-receptive College of Liberal Arts. Our faculty had long pushed for that move, and when the accreditation team incorporated this request into their report, the central administration adopted it. There were still close ties to the School of Business, for students who preferred the B.S.J. degree, but other students were more comfortable with liberal arts courses and a wider choice of electives.

During this time the mass communications industries were pushing to develop staffs that better reflected the country's diversity. We did what we could to let talented African American kids know they would be welcomed in the newsrooms. We secured a modest grant from the Newspaper Fund, enough to permit a bright undergraduate, Otis Sanford, and me to travel the state talking to high school students about journalism. Otis was a fine ambassador—he would later become managing editor of the Memphis *Commercial Appeal*. We like to think we changed a few minds, for we did recruit some promising students. We didn't get enough of them, but we tried.

Gale Denley, who ran our Scholastic Press Association, was a great help. One of our best recruits was Rose Jackson. Mary Lynn Kotz, an Ole Miss alumna who was a star in Washington journalism, said of Rose, "this is a woman who's going to amount to a great deal." As, indeed, she did.

A great strength of Ole Miss has always been the continuing support of its alumni. A superb example is James A. Autry, who at that time was editor of *Better Homes & Gardens*. Jere Hoar had kept in touch with him and was instrumental in getting Jim back to the campus. Jim had virtually invented a new approach to magazines, something he called "service journalism." Later he and his company, the Meredith Publications Group, hired Ole Miss graduates and funded magazine projects that led to national prominence for the program. Like Jim, many other alumni have remained emotionally (and financially) invested in the program and the university. Few institutions have been better served by the continuing loyalty and affection of their graduates.

Jere Hoar was interim chairman when I arrived at Ole Miss. His wife Betty quickly became a close friend to Gayla, who also got along well with Lib Fortune, the chancellor's wife. We had wonderful neighbors, Ed Dolan, a Harvard Ph.D. and a professor of classics, was a bright and engaging friend. Robert Khayat was my Sunday School teacher at the Methodist church. His kids, along with those of Ole Miss Athletics Director Warner Alford, were growing up with mine. Beyond that, the *Daily Mississippian* had its own thing going. Its staff bonded into a close-knit family, and those young people worked hard and played hard. At the end of each semester Lee White, the publisher, would throw a party at his cabin near Sardis Lake. We on the faculty used to worry about automobile accidents among the students, coming as they did down that curvy, gravel, remote road from a place where the beer flowed freely. But the kids managed to take care of themselves. The *Daily Mississippian* represented the heart of the program and was a respected— and plainspoken—conscience of the university. I wasn't at Ole Miss during the Meredith story, but was not surprised to learn of the paper's courage and professionalism. It's a gutsy, independent paper that does the university

71

proud. Always has.

Unlike so many journalism schools depressed about media conditions, Ole Miss graduates seem confident about the future. Returning to the campus recently, I found the atmosphere both realistic and upbeat. "One thing we know how to do is to produce content, that is, news and information," a senior told me. "We may not know what platforms or formats will be used, but we know how to handle news and information, and there'll always be a demand for that. We're going to be okay." Young men and women like those coming out of Ole Miss and Missouri, people who can work with multiple media outlets, have good reason to be encouraged.

I wasn't looking to leave Ole Miss in 1977. I had not applied for another job. We had received accreditation. Also we had been granted permission to leave the shambles of Brady Hall for the magnificent, to us, old Law School building. Preliminary renovation money had been appropriated, thus nailing down the deal. Still, there was the constant uphill battle for funds. The program had grown, but the budget had not kept pace. One day, out of the blue, I got a phone call from an old friend, Dwight Teeter, then director of the School of Journalism at the University of Kentucky. Dwight had accepted an endowed professorship at the University of Texas and Kentucky had been searching for a year for a successor. "Come up and at least give us a look," he said. So I went, and was astonished when I was offered the directorship at almost double my salary. (Let me add that back then doubling my salary didn't take a whole bunch of money.) Gayla and I drove the kids to Bluegrass Country, which they liked, and I accepted the job.

It wasn't easy to leave Ole Miss. We had been well treated there, and we were deeply connected to the institution and the community. Our kids loved their schools, and my wife and I were sad to leave our colleagues and friends. As we drove out of Oxford we cried, all four of us.

EDITOR'S NOTE: When Ron Farrar retired, Congressman James E. Clyburn said this on the floor of the U. S. House of Representatives:

"Mr. Speaker, I rise today to pay tribute to Dr. Ronald T. Farrar of South Carolina on the occasion of his retirement from the College of Journalism and Mass Communications at the University of South Carolina. Dr. Farrar is the epitome of what a college professor should be, and he is respected and loved by faculty and students alike.

"Along with the many articles Dr. Farrar has authored and published, he has written such books as *Reluctant Servant* (Missouri, 1968), *Mass Media and the National Experience*, with John D. Stevens (Harper & Row, 1971), *College 101* (Peterson's Guides, 1985, 1988), *Mass Communication: An Introduction to the Field* (Brown, 1995), *The Ultimate College Guide* (Peterson's, 1996), and *Walter Williams: Journalist to the World* (Missouri,

1998).

"Dr. Farrar is deeply respected in the fields of journalism and academics. His expertise and talent have earned him commissions to write numerous articles and conduct national studies. He has been awarded various grants and certificates of achievement, including the Distinguished Service Medal for Research in Journalism in 1969 by the Society of Professional Journalists for *Reluctant Servant: The Story of Charles G. Ross*. From 1971 to 1973 he was a consultant for a continuing study of television audiences for the Public Broadcasting System. Faculties for the U. S. government, private sectors and journalistic associations have been privileged to have him serve on their boards.

"His long career achievements include the award of research grants from the Kaltenborn Foundation, U. S. Steel Foundation, Harry S. Truman Library Institute, Indiana Research Foundation, Kentucky Press Association, Kentucky Humanities Council, Sigma Delta Chi Foundation, University of Kentucky Research Foundation, University of South Carolina Research Foundation, Southern Regional Education Board and the Freedom Forum.

"Dr. Farrar was appointed Reynolds-Faunt memorial professor in 1986 and held that professorship until his retirement. He will now be recognized as Distinguished Professor Emeritus.

"Mr. Speaker, I ask you and my colleagues to join me today in honoring Dr. Ronald T. Farrar for the incredible service he has provided through a lifetime in the academic community. I sincerely thank him for his outstanding contributions, congratulate him on his recent retirement, and wish him good luck and Godspeed in his future endeavors."

Will Norton

The Builder

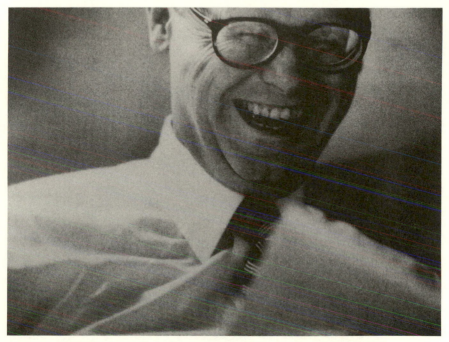

Will Norton, chair, Department of Journalism, 1979-1990.

"I come into a room and nobody notices," Will Norton likes to say. That is hardly the case, but what people do soon notice about Will Norton is his passionate commitment to journalism, to the First Amendment, and to journalism education. And his energetic and determined leadership.

When Will Norton took over the department at Ole Miss in 1977, he inherited a faculty of four housed in the homely, rundown frame house that was Brady Hall. The decision had already been made to relocate the unit to Farley Hall, what had been the Law School, but that move would not come to pass for some time. The curriculum was limited and narrowly focused on newspapers. Some 170 students were majoring in journalism. When he left Ole Miss in 1990, the faculty had grown to eight, full-time, along with several part-time adjunct professors, with a student enrollment of more than 350 majors. These young men and women could gain rigorous study and practice in an expanded curriculum that now included the areas of radio/television, advertising and public relations, as well as the continuing instruction in newspapers. Each area was well taught, though the faculty was still understaffed by at least two full positions. And—a rarity among journalism programs—Ole Miss also had added a sequence for magazine writers and editors and managers, which attained much national and international recognition. The department was far better situated in Farley Hall, a large, imposing presence on the Grove. The department's standing, both professionally and academically, was eminently respectable.

1990 *Daily Mississippian* senior staff: Jeremy Weldon, sports editor; Amy Stewart, assignments editor; Sonya Mason, news editor; Joe Gurner, entertainment editor; Lee Eric Smith, campus page editor; Bill Dabney, editor-in-chief; Clif Lusk, editorial page editor.

Much the youngest member of the journalism faculty when he was named chairman, Norton proved to be an innovative and capable manager, a man equipped with deep reserves of energy and determination. "Will grew in that job," recalls a newspaper friend. "It was gratifying to watch."[80] He gained visibility in both academic and professional circles and was soon known to be chairing a journalism program that was fast becoming one of the best in the region.

Hugo Wilbert Norton, Jr., was born in what was then the Ubangi territory of the Belgian Congo (now Zaire) in the darkest days of World War II. The leader of the Free French, Charles DeGaulle, was not far away, having fled from the Nazis to exile in Brazzaville, across the Congo from what was then

76

Leopoldville (now Kinshasa). Young Will—he never was fond of Hugo, an old Swedish family name—was the son of missionary parents.

Like many journalism professors, Will Norton took a circuitous route into the academy. He got his B.A., with honors, from Wheaton and worked for a time as sports editor of the *Wheaton Daily Journal*. He then went for his master's degree in journalism from Indiana University and followed this with three years on the staff of the *Chicago Tribune*. He left the *Trib* to join Christian Life Publications before enrolling in the doctoral program at the University of Iowa.

Norton by now had developed two beliefs that would guide him throughout the rest of his life. The first was a love for liberty. He learned that from seeing his father battle for religious freedom for his followers in the jungles and villages of Sub-Saharan Africa. The other was a love for journalism. His father helped him with that, too. "When we moved to a town, our father would take us to the newspaper each time," he recalls. "So we understood that a newspaper was important for the town." Good journalists generally need good journalism teachers. He had settled on a career path.

His doctorate in hand, young Will Norton joined the journalism faculty at the University of Mississippi in 1977. His colleagues, strong teachers who considered teaching, as opposed to research, their primary job, found Norton a well-prepared, hard-working individual who asked a great deal, and usually got it, from his students.

His passion for good journalism was infectious. "I distinctly remember one red-faced rant of Dr. Norton's," recalls Susan Griffing Christensen, ('79). "One of my classmates had done a sloppy job on a sports story for the *Daily Mississippian*, and Dr. Norton was livid. I remember thinking: (1) I don't ever want to get on Dr. Norton's bad side, and (2) there's no excuse for not caring whether you've got your facts straight. Teachers like Dr. Norton made me realize the standards of journalism are not to be taken lightly. And it's a profession worth being passionate about."[81]

Amy Carlisle DeLuca ('90), who became a TV reporter, remembers "Dr. Norton scared us to death with his 'pop quizzes' on current news events, but helped us realize how important it was to be informed about our state and our world.... I was adequately prepared and found the Ole Miss journalism program far superior to others that friends were involved with at the time."[82]

Nell Luter Floyd ('79), shares this experience: "My favorite memory centers around when I realized I was going to flunk Advanced Reporting. I knew well into the semester I was going to flunk because I was failing to meet the requirements that Will Norton had laid out, but I had put off breaking the news to my father. I called him and told him I wanted to change my major to something easier.... My father wouldn't hear of it and strongly suggested I take the class for a second time.... I did take Advanced Reporting for a second time and ended up with a B, almost an A. I look back and consider it a life lesson in persistence, certainly a good one for someone who ended up working as a newspaper reporter for 25 years."[83]

1979: The Department Of Journalism moved from Brady Hall to Farley Hall. (Photo by Kathy Ferguson)

Dr. Jere Hoar, who knew a thing or two about teaching, was so pleased with Will Norton's handling of Jere's son Tom that he wrote the dean, Gerald Walton, about it: "Will recognized an ability Tom had. . . directed him, encouraged him and salvaged him for journalism. I am confident that the attention Tom got was not because he is my son. It was because Will saw potential in him that other instructors had not seen, or if they had seen it had been unable to tap."[84]

Norton's concern for his students did not begin and end in his own classroom. One student, Robert Harter ('79), had the misfortune of taking his beginning reporting class with an instructor who taught poorly (the man was soon dismissed). "When I finally made it to Advanced Reporting," Harter said, "Dr. Norton took me aside and apologized for my having had to endure that professor. Until that time, I had no idea that anyone in the journalism department actually cared whether a student succeeded or not. From that moment on I realized that we were being mentored. I excelled in Advanced Reporting and got an A."[85]

In the spring of 1977, Ronald Farrar accepted a position as director of the School of Journalism at the University of Kentucky. That left the Ole Miss chairmanship open. Since two senior members of the faculty, Jere Hoar and Gale Denley, would be logical inside contenders for the job, the vice chancellor of academic affairs chose Will Norton, the most junior member of the faculty, to be interim chairman and to head the committee to conduct a national search for a permanent chairman. That search did not turn up any outstanding candidates. One or two finalists got invited to the campus, but did not impress. During this time, Norton had run the operation smoothly, and in his second year as interim the vice chancellor of academic affairs and the dean of liberal arts asked Norton to take the job on a permanent basis. Norton did not have tenure at the time, and he knew a chairmanship carried with it difficult, sometimes unpopular decisions. Well aware of the risks, he took on the job anyway.

"Looking back," a veteran journalist, Nell Luter, remembers, "I realize that Dr. Norton was the shot in the arm the department needed at the time."[86]

The records bear this out. In his first annual report as chairman, Norton wrote, in part:

> Enrollment was at a record 170 majors and more than 500 students. These numbers did not mean a loss of excellence. Journalism students were recognized campus-wide for their achievement with Taylor Medals and citations, Hall of Fame awards, etc. Moreover, some were recognized by national organizations. Rose Jackson, a black student from Clarksdale, was elected to the Society of Professional Journalists as a representative from one of four districts nationwide at the national convention. Mike Craft, a graduate student from Grenada, became the first journalism major from Ole Miss to be awarded a $3,000 scholarship to the Modern Media Institute in St. Petersburg, Fla.[87]

1979: *Daily Mississippian* newsroom. (Photo by Kathy Ferguson)

The next year reflected more growth and change. A public relations emphasis was developed and implemented. And merger talks continued as to who should—and could—handle the popular and important, but expensive, area of broadcasting.

The Department of Journalism had a legitimate interest in broadcast news. But broadcasting courses had been assigned to the Department of Speech and Theatre. For several years there had been student demand for a program in broadcast journalism, but broadcasting equipment was badly out of date, there was little money available to purchase new and updated cameras, editing equipment, and the like. Norton, like his predecessor as chairman, felt that the current broadcast program was too weak to survive an accreditation visit from the American Council on Education in Journalism and Mass Communications.

Eventually, however, broadcasting fell into Will Norton's lap. The Department of Speech and Theatre was increasingly focusing on acting and drama production courses and broadcasting was regarded as a drain and a liability. Norton was asked to take it over. Eventually, he agreed to do so, but stipulated that journalism be permitted to hire their own broadcast faculty. No additional funds were allocated in connection with this merger, at least not at first. It would take time and money and additional faculty, but Norton was determined to bring broadcast news up to accreditation—that is to say, professionally acceptable—standards.

A first step was to call in as a consultant one of the most respected figures

80

in journalism education, dean Neale Copple of the University of Nebraska, for an evaluation. Copple's recommendations gave Norton the ammunition he, and the central administration, needed to devise a broadcast news sequence, order new equipment, and hire the faculty expertise to make it all work. Copple's report read, in part,

> The merger of broadcasting into the journalism unit requires a search for therapy for the print-oriented faculty members, and some immediate decisions about space in the new quarters.

During his consulting visit, Copple talked to Ole Miss students, and in his report he went out of his way to praise them:

> … I was pleased with their apparent quality. They seemed bright, motivated, and loyal to the journalism program and the university. I was particularly pleased that you do not seem to have quite as much of the basic English problem as most of us do. I do not know your state well enough to know why, or even if, my assumption is true, but count your blessings.

It took a couple of years for broadcast news to gain strength.[88] In 1982 the hiring of Dr. James Pratt, a man with impressive academic as well as professional credentials, gave the broadcast sequence the quality leadership it needed. Within a few semesters, Ole Miss journalism graduates were landing jobs with radio and television stations throughout the region. And when the re-accreditation visit came around again, the broadcast sequence, like its older brother in print, became fully accredited. There was a proviso in the evaluation team's report, however, in that broadcasting needed more space. This report, along with the obvious need, helped get radio and television students and faculty the additional space and better equipment. Good things would follow. But, in typical Ole Miss fashion, unhurriedly.

During his tenure as chairman, Norton was able to add some excellent journalists to his teaching faculty. One of these was Jack Bass, who had been a reporter for 13 years and was twice named "Journalist of the Year" in South Carolina. His fame, however, rests on his books about events and personalities that helped shape southern history. He would write eight of these, each of which was well reviewed. One, a biography of Judge Frank M. Johnson Jr., won the Robert F. Kennedy award in 1994. David Broder, unofficial dean of the Washington Press Corps, described Bass's *Transformation of Southern Politics* as "a prime source for all those who follow Southern politics… a compelling story with insights on every page."[89] Though far better known as an author, Dr. Jack Bass was influential in the classroom also. "He made us read the *New York Times* and count how many words they used in a lead," recalls Bill Glenn ('92). ... He taught me two major things... as a journalism student: He helped my writing skills and he forced me to read the news."[90] After a few years at Ole Miss, Bass returned to his native South Carolina. He continued to write significant books, and when he retired from teaching he was named professor emeritus of humanities and social sciences at the College of Charleston.

The most famous of Norton's faculty recruits was Willie Morris, who arrived at Ole Miss in 1980. William Weaks Morris, the former editor in chief of *Harper's Magazine*, author of the prize-winning autobiography, *North Toward Home,* was known for his lyrical prose style. Morris was born in Jackson and grew up in Yazoo City. He attended the University of Texas where he was Phi Beta Kappa and the highly regarded editor of the university's student newspaper, the *Daily Texan.* He was awarded a Rhodes scholarship to Oxford University. In 1959 he became the editor of *The Texas Observer.* He joined the staff of *Harper's Magazine* in 1963 as Associate Editor and four years later was named editor-in-chief. He helped launch the careers of such notable writers as Larry L. King, William Styron and Norman Mailer. He became a media star, quoted in leading publications, giving speeches at prominent events and appearing regularly on television. In his years as editor he appeared eight times on the *Today Show*. In 1971 he left the magazine and moved to Long Island, living in a community of leading writers.

1979: Larry Wells, Willie Morris, Dean Faulkner Wells and Adam Shaw. (Photo by Walt Mixon)

Morris probably would not have been hired at Ole Miss if not for the initiative of Larry and Dean Faulkner Wells. The Oxford couple, writers and owners of Yoknapatawpha Press, met Willie in the spring of 1979 at the Greenwood Arts Festival. Willie was immediately drawn to them. As William Faulkner's niece, Dean represented the highest traditions of literature. "He made us his representatives at Ole Miss that day," Larry Wells recalls. "He asked us to meet him in November at the Sense of Place Symposium at USM. During that visit he asked us to speak to Chancellor Fortune in his behalf. He was ready to come home."

Ole Miss had not planned to have a writer-in-residence, had never had one, and the Department of English had no funds in their budget for a special lecture program. Norton contributed $7,000 to Morris' salary fund, and Dean and Larry Wells headed a fund drive that ultimately raised the money for the first year's salary.

"After the money was raised," Wells remembers, "Willie began thinking, 'Can I actually stand to live in Mississippi at its slow pace?' He was used to the Hamptons with his close circle of friends. We invited Willie down for a football weekend, and tailgated in the Grove. At the tailgating was Thad Cochran, the U.S. Senator; artist Bill Dunlap; E. Grady Jolly, later a justice on the United States Court of Appeals for the Fifth Circuit, and his wife, Bettye; Will and Patty Lewis, owners of Neilson's; Ed Morgan, owner of Morgan's Furniture on the Square and the son of Shine Morgan; Billy Ross Brown and his wife Lynn; and Dean and me. I got Walt Mixon to take a photo of us. Willie had a ball. He had not been to a tailgating party since his days at the University of Texas in Austin. Where he lived out on the east end of Long Island they had no college football, much less SEC football, and we were playing Georgia that day. Willie loved it. After the game Will and Patty gave a cocktail party, and afterwards we took him to Taylor Grocery. This was Willie's scouting trip to see if he could stand to live in Mississippi. When he got to town the first thing we did was take him to Rowan Oak. It was midnight and the house was closed and dark, but it was a beautiful night, and we toasted Mr. Bill with Mr. Jack Daniel. Willie had a wonderful time that weekend, and his friend, Adam Shaw, who had accompanied him to Mississippi, told him, 'If you don't come here, you're crazy. These people are great.'"

1979: Tailgating in the Grove are (l-r, seated) Willie Morris, E. Grady Jolly, Bettye Jolly; (l-r, standing) Bill Dunlap, Ed Morgan, Thad Cochran, Adam Shaw, Larry Wells, Dean Wells, Carl Downing, William Lewis. (Photo by Walt Mixon)

Willie began his ten-year tenure at Ole Miss teaching in the English Department. He brought well-known writers to speak to his American novels class: George Plimpton, John Knowles, William Styron, Gloria Jones, widow of James Jones, Winston Groom, Larry L. King, Ed Yoder and others.

Wells observes, "When he went to meet his first class with Pete, his Labrador retriever, students ran ahead of him to get a good seat. Willie's arrival on campus created genuine excitement at Ole Miss. I had never seen that kind of passion for *belles lettres*. When he got to the auditorium in Bishop Hall the place was packed. Pete lay down on the stage and Willie started to teach. Thus began a new era at Ole Miss."

Norton found out that Willie wanted to move to the Department of Journalism and readily seized the opportunity. Somehow he found funding and welcomed Willie to Brady Hall, where he would continue teaching until 1990. Morris revived the defunct *Ole Miss Magazine*, and for two semesters made it perhaps the best college magazine in the country. He chose assignments suited to his students' skills and personalities and edited their articles himself, sometimes sitting up all night in his campus residence at 16 Faculty Row. "I learned to edit copy looking over Willie's shoulder at four in the morning," Wells remembers. "It didn't matter how much drinking had gone on, Willie had an other-worldly concentration. With a cut here, a word added there, he made the students' articles sing!"

Morris' influence was felt beyond the classroom. He began to write about Ole Miss and Oxford, and brought the university and town to the attention of people throughout the nation. "Willie was a single-handed literary machine," says Wells. "He brought New York chic to Oxford. In 1983 when Billy 'Dog' Brewer was hired as head football coach at Ole Miss, Morris wrote a story for the *New York Times* called 'The Dog Comes Home.' He affectionately called Billy's wife Kay, 'Mrs. Dog.' He wrote for *TV Guide* about Ed Morgan's furniture store on the Square. He told about the ins and outs of Oxford, about people in all branches of life. In his personal life, he brought panache and style to Oxford. He was an inspired and compulsive storyteller, and absolutely obsessed with playing practical jokes. People sought him out. One time we were having dinner at the Gumbo Company, a restaurant where City Grocery is now, and Willie was asked to give a toast. It happened all the time. We would be sitting at a table, and he would whisper to Dean and me, 'Uh-oh, boss, please don't listen. And he would go over to a table and give some expansive, nostalgic and lyrical toast which rolled off the tip of his tongue. We had a great time with Willie."

Willie Morris retired from teaching in 1990 and moved to Jackson, but his influence on Oxford and Ole Miss can still be felt today.

Another important addition to the Department of Journalism was Tommy Miller, whom Norton hired from the *Houston Chronicle* in 1981. He proved to be a tough, demanding teacher and an imposing presence in the classroom. "From the beginning of the semester it quickly became apparent that this was not an ordinary class and Tommy Miller was not an ordinary teacher," wrote Lyn Heard McMillan ('85). "Fresh from the *Houston Chronicle*, Mr. Miller brought real-world experience to our very sheltered environment that was Ole Miss and Oxford. He . . . constantly encouraged us to see a bigger picture."[91]

Kitty Dumas ('84), remembers: "I always thought of Tommy Miller as a kind of newspaper god, a newspaperman's newspaperman. Movies were made about guys like that. Tough, relentless, wily as hell. He was a guy from the big city who could get a story anywhere. I wanted to be a guy like that."[92]

But after a few years in the classroom, Miller was lured back to the *Houston Chronicle,* where he ultimately became managing editor. In 2011, he lost his battle to a long illness, and his passing evoked dozens of sympathy messages from the Ole Miss students he had taught and inspired more than two decades before.

The magazine sequence, developed on Norton's watch at Ole Miss, would be one of the relatively few in the nation and certainly one of the best known. Like so much else in the history of journalism at Ole Miss, the process started with one of its own, a loyal alumnus.

Of all the Ole Miss journalism graduates who starred as professional journalists, James A. Autry is among the most illustrious. An early graduate of the program—he was one of Gerald Forbes' first undergraduate majors—Jim Autry early on got into the magazine field. He moved up through the ranks at the Meredith Publishing Co. of Des Moines, becoming editor of Meredith's leading publication, *Better Homes and Gardens*. Along the way he developed a reporting style he came to call "service journalism,"[93] providing assistance to the reader as well as information.

Proud of his Ole Miss roots, Jim Autry came back to the campus on occasion to do guest lectures, and in the process he and Will Norton became friends. Norton, who early in his career had done magazine work, had revived *Mississippi Magazine* in 1975 and that year it was judged the outstanding student magazine in the four-state region. In time, *Mississippi Magazine* would again fold for lack of funding. But Norton remained convinced that magazine journalism belonged in the department's curriculum, and Jim Autry's ideas on service journalism struck him as a promising springboard. Norton proposed that the Meredith Corporation establish a model magazine program and locate it at the University of Mississippi. Autry agreed. Norton then worked up a proposal and in November 1983, he presented it to Meredith's chief executive officer, Robert Burnett.

"After the presentation," Norton recalled later, "Autry broke the silence, earnestly endorsing it with his full backing. I will never be able to forget the warm feeling of relief that came with those words."[94]

Armed with Meredith funding, Norton was able to hire someone to set up the magazine curriculum and make it work. A top official at Meredith, like Will Norton, had been impressed by a doctoral student at the University of Missouri, Samir Husni, who was rapidly building a reputation for reporting on the dozens of new magazines that were constantly entering the field. Norton's discussions with Husni's professors at Missouri led to what turned out to be a spectacularly successful hire. Husni, now Dr. Husni, brought with him the energy and expertise that would make the Ole Miss program nationally famous. And earn for Husni the nickname "Mr. Magazine."[95]

Welcome as it was, the Meredith funding alone could not solve the larger budgetary problems, which grew more acute year after year. Though racking up healthy increases in student numbers and the credit hours, the department urgently needed more financial support. Instead, it got less. The cuts were severe enough to prompt the academic vice chancellor, Peter E. Wagner, to fire off an impassioned memo to his boss, executive vice chancellor Harvey S. Lewis:

... We have picked the Journalism Department clean.... We cannot deprive them of one more penny if we wish to maintain a robust department.... I cannot think of language strong enough to convey my concern that the journalism department might unintentionally be penalized.... I beg you to protect the surviving journalism budget at all costs.... Will (Norton) is breaking his back to be cooperative....[96]

Then disaster, or what certainly seemed like it, struck from another, and totally unexpected, quarter.

Unlike most universities, Ole Miss did not have its own governing board. Instead, all the colleges and universities in Mississippi were controlled by a central agency, the Board of Trustees of Institutions of Higher Learning. In the autumn of 1981, the board decided to minimize duplication among various schools by designating what it called "leadership" in specific areas. Under this plan, no degree programs would be terminated, but priority, notably for planning and funding purposes, would go to the program deemed to have "leadership" in that area. There were three so-called comprehensive universities to deal with—Ole Miss, Mississippi State University, and the University of Southern Mississippi—and the board wanted to share the wealth, as it were, in assigning "leadership" roles.

The central administration at Ole Miss was well aware of the historic and fundamental importance of the liberal arts—the school was founded as a liberal arts college—and was determined to preserve "leadership" in the liberal arts areas. Hanging on to liberal arts came at a price, however, and that price was seeing "leadership" in some other areas go elsewhere.

1986: *Daily Mississippian* staff (back row), Bobby Pepper, Miles Marcus, Alan McCracken, Johnny Weathersby, Bo Bean, Rob MLeod, Billy Moak; middle Row Meg Moellenhoff, Renee Gammil, Susie Hoover, Bill Moore, Kim Bryant, Toni Lepeska, Rhonda Gooden, Debbie Kloha, Jane Hill; front row: Katie Smith, Beth Shaw, Karl Floyd, Tara Jennings.

Journalism got thrown under the bus. "Leadership" in communications, including journalism, was assigned to the University of Southern Mississippi, despite the fact that the only nationally accredited journalism program in Mississippi was at Ole Miss.

Ole Miss journalism alumni were stung, more than a few were outraged, at the board's decision. And if the central administration at Ole Miss would not go to the mat for journalism, friends and alumni of the program would. Many wrote letters of protest. One, from Jim Autry, by now general manager of magazine operations at Meredith Publishing, said this:

> We (alumni) believe the board of trustees made a serious error in failing to designate the University of Mississippi as a lead institution in journalism. And we are concerned that, as a result of this failure, the only demonstrably superior journalism program in the state of Mississippi will atrophy and, perhaps, die.
>
> We seek not to disparage the other institutions of higher learning, but clearly there is one outstanding journalism program in the state of Mississippi. Clearly there is one journalism program which has produced the most outstanding journalists in

the state, and many of the most outstanding journalists in the South and in the nation. Clearly there is one journalism program which has a long history of balanced academic discipline and practical professional training. And clearly there is one journalism program which should continue to grow and should, with proper support and planning, achieve its rightful status as a school of journalism.

That program is at Ole Miss.[97]

In addition to powerful letters, perhaps even more effective, was the, forceful, one-on-one politicking done by friends and alumni with the board of trustees. Newspaper publishers, political campaign managers and others with strong ties to Ole Miss journalism —and no small measure of influence— made their case. When the 1983-84 academic year began, the board of trustees, quietly and without opposition, reversed itself and declared Ole Miss the state's leader in journalism. A potentially lethal bullet had been dodged.

1986: Debbie Kloha, *Daily Mississippian* editor

Loyal and emotional support, however, was one thing, while funding was quite another. The central administration had made it clear to Will Norton that his department, though nationally accredited and a valuable asset to the campus, simply would not be prominent in the long-range planning for the University of Mississippi, and certainly not destined to develop into a School of Journalism. That dreary realization not only shattered a dream, it caused Norton to believe he had done about all he could do at Ole Miss.

Job offers, and feelers and invitations to apply elsewhere, had been coming with some frequency to Will Norton, whose enthusiastic and effective leadership by now had become known throughout the relatively small world of academic journalism. In 1990, he reluctantly decided it was time to move on.

The most tempting offer was to replace his friend Neale Copple, who was retiring as dean of the College of Journalism and Mass Communications at the University of Nebraska. Nebraska had gotten into journalism early on, and over the years had built a large, well-funded operation that commanded statewide and national respect. Copple's program was short on theory and long on professionalism, a view Norton shared. Indeed, some of the nation's top journalists had learned their craft at Nebraska. It was the kind of energetic, hard-nosed journalism school Norton had envisioned for Ole Miss. Because of that, and because his salary would approximately double, Norton accepted the Nebraska deanship.

His resignation from Ole Miss created something of a stir, especially among Mississippi journalists. Many of them appreciated what he had been able to accomplish during his chairmanship, and many of them understood why he would be leaving. That winter, during a convention of the Mississippi Press Association in Jackson, friends and colleagues and alumni gathered for a good-natured roasting of Will Norton. The "roasters" lineup included Charles Overby, a top executive with Gannett Newspapers; Tommy Miller, a popular former faculty member who had gone to the *Houston Chronicle*; Charlie Mitchell, editor of the *Vicksburg Post*, Ruth Ingram of the Jackson *Clarion-Ledger*, and Mike Austin, an attorney at McComb. Also attending, perhaps stemming from a sense of guilt for not working harder to keep his journalism chairman, was Dr. Gerald Turner, chancellor of the university. The gentle "roasting" made for a good evening, and before the night was out there came a most dramatic, and most welcome, announcement: The Cook Foundation would be awarding $1 million to journalism at Ole Miss. It was the largest gift the program had ever gotten at that time, and a revealing acknowledgement of the respect Will Norton and his faculty and alumni had earned. Norton's 14 years as chairman had been productive and rewarding, but it was time to go.

One day, much later, he would come back.

By 2009, Norton had been at Nebraska for 19 years and, in fact, was the longest-serving dean on that campus. He had reached retirement age, and though the central administration at Nebraska wanted him to stay on, he decided it was time to step aside. Not only that, but to leave Lincoln so as to give the new dean room to maneuver without worrying about any backseat driving from his predecessor.

But Norton had no intention of retiring.

At Ole Miss, an old friend and former colleague, Ed Meek, had donated millions to Ole Miss, enough money to establish and maintain a School of Journalism. To take over as the school's first dean, the university administration offered the post to Will Norton. Though well into his 60s, Norton had plenty of energy left. His father was still teaching at 88. So, in a remarkable about-face, Will Norton came back to Ole Miss. In his heart, he had never left.

Don Sneed

The Office Door is Open

Don Sneed, chair, Department of Journalism, 1991-1994.

"Eighty percent of the work of a university administrator can be done by a six-year-old," the Provost of Indiana University once observed. "It's that other 20 percent that we worry about."

He was joking, but there was some truth in what he said. The "eighty percent" to which he referred was the routine—completing endless administrative forms, making out schedules, presiding at faculty and committee meetings. The successful administrator earned the pay, and kept the job, by how well he or she performed in that "other 20 percent:" maneuvering within the academic bureaucracy, managing relations not only with students and faculty but with parents, academic higher-ups and, in journalism, with the professional community in the mass media.

It was "that other 20 percent" that made Don Sneed miserable.

When he was hired as chairman of the Ole Miss Department of Journalism in 1991, he came in with perhaps the most impressive academic and professional credentials of anyone who ever held that job. He had presented some 36 papers at professional conferences and published 60 articles in scholarly and professional journals. He had recently been named outstanding journalism professor at San Diego State University. He also had ten years of newspaper

91

him, including stints at the *Hattiesburg American* and
ibune. Besides his scholarly writing, he had published op-
in some big-time metro dailies, including the *Boston Globe*,
, Los Angeles Times, Chicago Tribune and various others. He
.t, a proven scholar and teacher who had shown he could hold his
.op professional journalists anywhere.
Donald Sneed, who held a doctorate from Southern Illinois University,
red after an exhaustive, nine-month, national search. The search was
.ult—a nice problem to have, because there had been quite a few strong
.plicants. Will Norton's leadership had put Ole Miss on the map, and the
department of Journalism had become known as an attractive place to be.
Eventually the applicants were screened down to five, and both the search
committee and the journalism faculty votes were split.

Two things most likely persuaded the administration to settle on Don
Sneed. One was his extraordinary scholarship. Like most universities, Ole
Miss was seeking national recognition as an institution where faculty produced
and published scholarly research. Sneed was enormously successful in that
area, and the hope was that he would serve as a role model to mentor and
motivate some others on the faculty to publish. Few were doing research at all,
and fewer still were getting their by-lines into the scholarly and professional
journals. Then there was another, and perhaps even more important, point
in Don Sneed's favor: Timing. In two years, the journalism department at
Ole Miss would have to undergo a re-accreditation visit. Gaining national
accreditation for journalism at Ole Miss had not been easy; the institution
was proud of the accreditation and determined to keep it. Don Sneed had
just navigated San Diego State through its re-accreditation, with all that had
required in terms of preparation and savvy. If accreditation was a game, Don
Sneed knew how to play it.

1992: *Daily Mississippian* advertising staff (left to right): John Jordan, Stephanie Mitchell, Jean Larroux. *In jeep*: Beverly Prince and Oliver "Ollie" Brock. *Center:* Beverly Brown, Shannon Spears, Ashley Sims. *Back row:* Joel Ewing, Melanie Wadkins, Salita Bryant, Cathy Still, Nancy Byrd.

As hoped and expected, during Sneed's first year scholarly production went up considerably. Sneed himself published a book, *The Publisher-Public Official: Real or Imagined Conflict of Interest?*[98] along with several conference papers and journal articles. Several other faculty members were awarded research grants and broke through with publications in scholarly journals.

Dr. Ed Meek, an associate professor on a part-time basis, landed a $4.5 million grant from the Mississippi Department of Human Services for what was called "Project Leap: Learn, Earn and Prosper," an ambitious program to fund a satellite network origination from the Ole Miss campus, using talent from around the nation to teach basic literacy to men and women who were unemployable.

Dr. Samir Husni became increasingly prominent as a magazine consultant, developing high visibility, both as a writer and as the subject of national interviews. Dr. Jack Bass, a brilliant reporter whose books had received national acclaim, was now recognized as an authoritative spokesman on race relations and Southern politics. Prof. Joe Atkins published articles in several regional and national journals as well as dozens of op-ed columns in the Jackson *Clarion-Ledger*, *Hattiesburg American* and other newspapers. Dr. Jere Hoar, who held emeritus rank but still had an office on campus, published more fiction pieces, all well received.[99]

Don Sneed was off to a good start.

For all his scholarship, however, Sneed remained at heart a teacher—an energetic and creative teacher at that. *Editor & Publisher*, then the nation's leading trade journal for the newspaper field, wrote of Sneed: "Students and colleagues alike remember Sneed as an inventive, hands-on teacher who paired 'nuts-and-bolts' instruction with constant guidance and encouragement.[100]

One of his teaching innovations was to develop a video report card: That is, videotaping an in-depth evaluation of each student's work for that semester.

"It's so tempting, at the end of a long semester, to just add up a student's grades, write them down on paper and then go fishing," Sneed said. "We're in the information age now, and with all that technology, we can give a lot more information than you can ever fit on a printed card."

Sneed's video report cards, which he had begun at San Diego State, had inspired features in the *Los Angeles Times* and the *New York Times*. National Public Radio and many local and national television reporters interviewed him about his unique teaching methods.[101]

The tape he prepared for each student ran 20 to 25 minutes and was a detailed discussion of strengths and weaknesses the professor had found. "They're not all glowing reports," Sneed said. "I'll point out the warts and blemishes, talk about the mechanics of their writing, whether or not they pay attention to style or grammar, and read some of their work aloud."

The tapes were described as "long on substance and short on theatrics." Indeed, Sneed recorded many of the tapes in his back yard, with his wife operating the camera and birds singing in the background.

Despite the homely production values, the tapes received generally favorable reviews, not only from the students but also from their parents.

The video report cards were optional, and not every student wanted one, preferring to get the usual print version. And not many professors wanted to switch over to the video route.

"The idea hasn't exactly caught fire," Sneed conceded. "I don't advocate that teachers adopt this grading method. It's labor-intensive, and it takes hours to put the tapes together. By the time you're finished, you're dead tired."[102]

He was of medium height and weight, with a high forehead and gray, wavy hair. He was usually outfitted in a dress shirt and tie, but rarely a jacket. His manner was mild, even diffident, in conversation.[103] He was much tougher in his written e-mails and notes to faculty.

Too, he seemed to identify comfortably with Mississippi journalism and was keenly interested in their operations. He visited newspaper offices around the state, sometimes writing about them afterward.

He pushed himself hard. And, always lurking in the background, was the forthcoming re-accreditation visit, which required a massive self-study, and compilation of virtually everything the unit had done since the last visit. The self-study book, to be filled with data and might extend to several hundred pages, would be carefully examined by the team of academics and professionals who would later conduct an on-site visit. The on-site visit was crucial, especially to a unit struggling to manage with less than ideal resources.

But accreditation can be won or lost on the quality and thoroughness of the self-study book. Sneed knew how the system worked, knew that the on-site team members might well have made up their minds about Ole Miss journalism after reading the self-study book and long before they ever arrived on the campus.

The pace began to tell. Sneed became less and less patient with the university's bureaucracy, and he quarreled openly with various colleagues and administrators. He was especially angry with the Graduate School and its stringent standards. The Graduate School's admission policies and degree requirements did not bend — at least where Sneed was concerned.

(It should be noted that at many institutions of higher learning there are department chairmen and other administrators who have suffered bloody noses from losing fights with their own Graduate Schools, which seem to be universally inflexible. As an example, the provost of the University of Kentucky once grumbled that "the entire graduate program of this university is controlled by two little old ladies. One doesn't want to let anybody in and the other doesn't want to let anybody out.")

Sneed's feuds, especially over the Graduate School's policies, soon became ugly and personal, affecting, among much else, faculty and staff morale. Worse still, it overshadowed the good work being done by some key figures in the department. Dr. Ed Meek by now had been awarded $7 million in grants to sustain his statewide satellite network campaign from the Oxford campus to combat illiteracy. Dr. Samir Husni's observations on the magazine industry received big-media national attention as well as a highly favorable profile in the respected *Chronicle of Higher Education*. Dr. Jack Bass continued to reach appreciative audiences with his writings and speeches on Southern politics and race relations issues. Other less visible faculty members were also quietly producing articles for research and professional journals. Teaching quality remained high.

Re-accreditation was granted that spring of 1993. The on-site team did not give the unit a perfect score, but found strengths at Ole Miss that more than made up for shortcomings in budget and equipment and other resources. Sneed had done what he had been hired to do.

But he had had it with administration at Ole Miss. It was that "other 20 percent" of the job that exacted a more painful price than he was prepared to pay. He had been wounded emotionally, and though many of the wounds were self-inflicted, they still hurt. After one too many battles, many of them with the Graduate School, he resigned in 1994—not "with regret" but with an expression of great joy. "I'm free at last! Free at last!" he told friends.[104]

He made his way to Florida International University, and found it an agreeable environment where he could do what he did best, teach and write. He spent his summers working at newspapers around the nation, keeping his hand in and his ideas fresh. The North Dakota Newspaper Association awarded him a first place for editorial writing in 2004.   His dean at Florida International, Dr. Lillian Lodge Kopenhaver, said he was a very successful teacher, happy in his work and much admired by his students.[105] Students especially praised his "open door" policy, which meant he was freely available for a consultation, or for a mentoring session, or simply to talk about journalism. This was rare, and was appreciated. Throughout the academy, too many professors closet themselves inside their offices, ostensibly correcting papers or working on their research, minimizing, even ignoring, contact with students outside the classroom.

In late October, 2005, while hard at work on another book, Don Sneed died of a heart attack at his home in Plantation, Florida. He was three days shy of his 61st birthday.

The next day, his office door on the Florida International campus was opened, as it would have been, to welcome those honoring his memory. His faculty colleagues did that for him, and it was just the kind of gesture he would have wanted.[106]

Stuart Bullion

A Gentleman and a Scholar

Stuart Bullion, chair, Department of Journalism, 1997-2004.

After the abrupt resignation of Don Sneed in 1994, the top administrators at Ole Miss once again turned over the reins of the Department of Journalism to Dr. Samir Husni, who had proven a capable and trusted leader. His professional agenda already crowded with his growing and nationally prominent magazine program, Husni would serve as interim chairman for two years, then was made chairman in1996 while the national search for a permanent chairman dragged on.

In 1997, the searchers finally found the man they wanted, Dr. Stuart James Bullion. At the time, he had chaired the journalism program at the University of Maine, of all places, but few individuals had deeper, and more affectionate, associations with Oxford and Ole Miss. His mother, Maralyn Howell Bullion, was an Oxford native who, remarkably, became the first female to be elected president of the Ole Miss student body. His grandfather had served as clerk of the Lafayette County Chancery Court. A cousin, Paul Howell, had been editor of the *Daily Mississippian* in 1978-79. His family ties to Mississippi went back to the 1800s.

An army brat, Stuart Bullion had been born in Minnesota but lived in Oxford as a boy. He got his bachelor's degree at Princeton, where he had studied French language and culture. Drafted into the Army after graduation, he served in Vietnam, a foot soldier in the famed 101st Airborne Division, which had been tasked with patrolling the Khe Sanh area. It was the scene of some of the bloodiest combat of the war, and Bullion came in for more than his share of it.

After his discharge, he wanted to return to Princeton to seek a Ph.D in French literature. However, he was warned that the anti-military sentiment was so intense and pervasive among the French Department faculty at Princeton that he, or any returning veteran, would find it virtually impossible to get past an examining committee and earn his doctorate there.[107] He then enrolled at the University of Minnesota, intending to study French literature, but soon decided, as he put it, to do something more active. He found a job on a community newspaper in Minnesota. "I got to do everything," he said of that weekly. "I reported, edited, shot photos and laid out pages." Before long he had been made editor and was winning awards from the Minnesota Press Association. In the process he had come to love the field of journalism, and, stemming from that, a desire to impart that love to students. He went back to Minnesota for graduate study in journalism and the beginning of a teaching career.[108]

1997: *Daily Mississippian* staff (standing left to right), Chrissy Hall, photo editor; Melanie Simpson, managing editor; Jamie Kornegy, entertainment editor; Marty Sewell, sports editor; Rebecca J. Lauck, entertainment assistant; Mandy Jones, news editor; Jenny Dodson, copy editor; (seated) Rob Robertson, editor.

Eventually, by way of teaching stints at Spring Hill College, two branches of Southern Illinois University, and eight years at Maine, he arrived at Ole Miss. "I have had my eye on the University of Mississippi since I was in graduate school," he said. "On visits to Oxford, I never failed to check to see if there were any openings in the (journalism) department. Quite frankly, this is a dream come true."[109]

"We needed someone to take us into the 21st century," said Dr. Husni, relieved to shed his duties as temporary chairman and return to building his magazine program. "Hopefully, this is the guy."[110]

Enthusiastic supporters at Ole Miss were hoping, and perhaps expecting, Stuart Bullion to immediately create a School of Journalism. Or, at the very least, a "Center for Mass Communications Leadership."

Bullion, however, urged caution. To his friend Ed Meek, Bullion wrote:

> As I understand the history of the 'school of journalism' aspirations, there is consensus that the existing unit lacks the physical size to become a self-sustaining school.... More critical, in my opinion, is the need to first establish a valid national reputation for excellence in journalism and mass communi-cation teaching, service and research. As a member of AEJMC, and having studied and taught journalism on four campuses, I can tell you that Ole Miss does not yet have that reputation 'out there.' I do believe the department's reputation in fact lags behind the unit's actual quality, but that discrepancy must be corrected in a well-planned and well-executed campaign.... I believe the department has a ways to go in overall quality of teaching, research and service— as well as physical size—to be able to aspire to a status of 'school' or 'center.'[111]

Bullion knew what needed to be done, and he set about doing it.

His first year, he took the final payment to fill out the Cook Foundation's million-dollar gift to the school to endow a chaired professorship. Sid Salter and John Johnson, both distinguished Mississippi newspapermen, held the chair for short periods. Salter was Perspective editor of the Jackson *Clarion-Ledger*, while Johnson, who had been the paper's editor, was also a recipient of the Pulitzer Prize.

Bullion oversaw the renovation of Farley Hall and managed to put through a slight revision of the curriculum, bringing it in more in line with industry changes. He also tackled the problem of racial diversity on his faculty. The first minority professor in journalism at Ole Miss was Ed Welch, who had been hired in 1979 to teach broadcasting. He resigned to pursue his Ph.D., and after that was conferred he went to the University of Memphis. Across the nation, journalism schools were competing for members of racial minorities to join their faculties, and at that time the pool of minority individuals who possessed media experience and graduate degrees was small. Dr. Flora McGhee was the second. Nevertheless, Bullion was able to add a third, associate professor

Burnis Morris. Other African American professors would follow as openings and availabilities permitted. Among universities, all hires seem to take a long time, and when position openings are few and the prospects to fill them relatively scarce, the process can move at a glacial pace.

Bullion also oversaw a successful re-accreditation review of the department in 1998.

Like many in the academy, Stuart Bullion was never comfortable as a fundraiser. "I don't like going around with a tin cup in my hand," he confided to a friend.[112] Nevertheless, the journalism program was awarded a $5 million grant from Charles Overby and the Freedom Forum, to build what became known as the Overby Center. Then, at Overby's urging, the chancellor, Robert Khayat, garnered another $500,000 from the legislature to renovate Farley Hall.[113]

Bullion's performance earned him high marks, especially from the administrative higher-ups at Ole Miss. "He brings strong credentials to the position, both academic and administrative," said Dr. Dale Abadie, dean of liberal arts, "as well as an enthusiasm and energy."[114]

Bullion was a polished, handsome man of average build. His dark hair was worn shorter than most, though not in a brush cut. He had a ready smile, a quick wit, and was good company.[115] His wife, Hahn, was Vietnamese, well schooled in French culture, and she shared her husband's love of French language and literature.[116]

In the classroom, he was always prepared and well organized, and he was able to blend touches of humor into his lectures. He typically wore a sweater vest, dress shirt and necktie and a blazer. Somewhat formal but at the same time relaxed, he easily blended humor into his lectures. "He would stand up there with the chalk in his hand," recalled one undergraduate, "and looked what one imagined a professor would look like." Another student wrote that Bullion was beloved by students as "the chair who cared."

His dedication and professionalism were reflected in his teaching. "I've learned that you have to get students passionately engaged in our field, because journalism is as much a lifestyle as a job," he said. "I learned that you have to be rigorous but fair in grading and advising, because your journalism degree has to be credible for the media industries."[117]

Students knew he was a stickler for high journalistic standards, but he confessed to one lapse: "My biggest professional ethics sin: I lied about my typing speed. I still hunt and peck."[118]

And though he was a solid supporter of the student newspaper's editorial freedom, he reserved the right to complain when he thought the paper had strayed off course. One *Daily Mississippian* editorial, as an example, took what he regarded as the wrong interpretation of an episode of racially inspired hooliganism, and prompted this stinging letter to the editor:

I commend you for your prompt, complete and continuing coverage of the ugly racist vandalism reported in Kincannon Hall Wednesday morning. I support you in your call for zero tolerance for the perpetrators, whose acts make them the most despised minority on our campus, and who have no place in the Ole Miss community.

I wish I could end my letter right here, but I cannot refrain from condemning your dishonest and self-righteous editorial on Nov. 7 ("Ole Miss still tainted").

It's one thing to insinuate that the *DM* is like some masked avenger engaged in a solitary campaign to expose racial incidents at Ole Miss. I'll credit that to a combination of youthful hubris and immature judgment.

It's quite another thing to mendaciously malign everyone who has helped plan and carry out this year's "Open Doors" observances on the occasion of the 40th anniversary of the desegregation of the university. You may target "Ole Miss administrators," but your broad brush besmirches everyone who gathered in front of the Lyceum Oct. 1 to remember an awful past and hope for a better future. I take your misguided fulmination personally; I was a member of the Open Doors planning committee....

What was your purpose in gratuitously trashing the faculty, students, staff and community members who dared to confront our university's past mistakes and pledge themselves to continued progress? Your conclusions are so ill-founded that the only credibility you damage is your own.[119]

Bullion cared deeply, and did not hesitate to align himself with causes, even unpopular ones. During the late '90s, a handful of zealots attempted to show their disdain for their country by burning an American flag. The public was outraged, and a serious, national effort developed to enact a Constitutional amendment that would make flag burning a criminal offense. Bullion wrote a long op-ed piece opposing such an amendment. The piece read, in part:

One can burn an American flag, but no one can defile the ideals for which it stands. Our flag waves no less proudly for the misguided actions of a few extremists. As long as Old Glory remains the people's flag, the American people will defend her, as they always have—without a Constitutional amendment.[120]

He was a private person, somewhat secretive, even about his own research projects. One topic of keen interest to him was mass media coverage of death

101

penalty and execution cases. He kept copious, coded notes, but, so far as is known, never developed a completed manuscript on that subject.

Like so many who had been a part of the bloody fighting in Vietnam, Bullion remained troubled by it long after he had returned to civilian life. He said little about his own experiences. Other vets were writing novels about the war, however, and Bullion found that trend distasteful. In a haunting, starkly revealing essay he wrote:

> I don't care for a lot of Viet Nam fiction because most of the authors feel compelled to editorialize about the rightness or the wrongness of being there. Maybe it's the journalist in me, but I start questioning the credibility of the work as a whole when I sense a self-conscious politicization....
>
> The book I'd really like to read would be written by Panama, nicknamed for his homeland, who enlisted to risk his life to gain U.S. citizenship. Panama barely spoke English, and we had to draw pictures in the dirt to communicate. I want to hear from Jitterbug, the inner city black kid whose touch on the machine gun was like a jazz drum solo. In the field, Jitterbug was a bosom buddy. But when we stood down to Camp Eagle for a few days, he had no choice but to join a rear-echelon soul-brother gang whose thing was to intimidate and sometimes assault white soldiers. I want to read what Angel would write. Angel, the tall, thin, blond point man with his love beads and peace symbols and his marijuana and his amphetamines and his heroin and his one tape of Crosby, Stills, Nash & Young's "D J Vu" and his hatred of lifers and his contempt for anyone who wasn't a head....
>
> I don't like reading about the war in general because of the repressed feelings that stir in me when I realize as I'm reading that my breath is coming faster, my stomach is tightening, my sentimentality is going into suspension. It's the adrenaline rush of the last 100 yards banking into an unsecured LZ[1] in the lead slick, when the door gunners on both sides let loose on the tree line. I learned how to feel like that when I had to, when I was a soldier once and young, but I don't need those feelings anymore, and they frighten me. They remind me of the things I'm carrying — that time and that place — and there's still a long hump ahead.[121]

Bullion knew the central administration at Ole Miss, as well as some journalism alumni, were aware that other institutions in the state were moving ahead with journalism programs of their own. The University of Southern

Mississippi at Hattiesburg had fashioned a mass communications unit and had obtained authority from the state board to offer the doctoral degree in that field. Jackson State, Mississippi University for Women, and Delta State, among others, had launched undergraduate courses in journalism. If it was to remain the state's leading journalism program, Ole Miss needed a special distinction.

So, perhaps against his better judgment, Bullion drafted in 1997 a proposal for a Journalism Center. Knowing his faculty was too small to staff a full-scale, broad-cased communications curriculum, Bullion wanted to draw upon other departments across the campus to provide a multidisciplinary approach. He wanted to name the Center for Charles Overby, who headed the Freedom Forum and was responsible for substantial financial support, and he hoped Al Neuharth, who headed Gannett Newspapers and preceded Overby at the Freedom Forum, would lend his considerable clout to the project.

The center proposal never got any traction, however, and as things progressed a turf battle arose within the campus bureaucracy. The issue arose as the Journalism Department's quarters in Farley Hall were being renovated. A top-level decision was made to remove the S. Gale Denley Media Center away from Farley Hall, where the Department of Journalism was housed, and across the campus to Bishop Hall. Bullion and his faculty protested, but in a letter to the provost, Thomas D. Wallace, the vice chancellor in the Office of Student Affairs, wrote:

> The Student Media Center at the University of Mississippi is a part of the Division of Student Life for good reason. The department consists of entities other than the *Daily Mississippian* and Channel 12. Also included are the Ole Miss Yearbook, *Oxford Health* and *Fitness Magazine*, the DM Online, Rebel Radio and the new converged media project. The DM employs approximately 100 students who work in editorial, 7 in circulation, 5 in production, and 6 in sales; Channel 12 employs 30 students, including on-air talent, writers, reporters, producers, directors, camera operators, and technicians; the Ole Miss Yearbook employs 20 students; Oxford Health and Fitness employs 10 students; Rebel Radio employs 45 students, including on-air talent, production, music direction, specialty shows, sports, news, and 6 students in sales.
>
> While the relationship between the journalism department and some parts of student media is symbiotic, the relationship between journalism and other aspects of student media is not . . .[122]

To the journalism faculty, it was a knife directed at the very heart of the journalism faculty's hopes and plans for the education and future of their students.

In a letter to the provost, Bullion tried to make his case:

> The reaction of my faculty is uniformly one of dismay and alarm, which I share. . . Since the journalism department was established in 1947, *The Mississippian* has served as a practical laboratory and as a publication outlet for work journalism majors produce for their classes. In more recent years, the television has served a parallel function for broadcast journalism students. Without a portfolio of work that has been produced or aired, our graduates cannot compete on the job market. . . I expect that our alumni would see the physical alienation of the *DM* and TV newsroom in the same way journalism faculty see it. If anything, they would react with greater alarm.

> What is being proposed is perhaps the most drastic action that has been taken in the 55 years of the Department of Journalism . . .[123]

But that train had already left the station. For the first time in its history, the Department of Journalism and the *Daily Mississippian* would not be under the same roof. It was a bitter pill.

Despite losing a vitally important turf war, the Department of Journalism continued to grow. The progress launched during the Will Norton years continued apace, and by 2003 Stuart Bullion thought the program had the size and, more importantly, the quality of faculty and students to justify not a center, but a School of Journalism.

In a carefully crafted proposal, Bullion stated the case:

> In recent years, the Department of Journalism has grown rapidly in size and complexity, with additional changes foreseen, to the point that it is appropriate for the unit to be re-designated a School of Journalism within the College of Liberal Arts. The professional nature of the B.A. degree program, while deeply rooted in the liberal arts, further justifies having a school —rather than a department of journalism. In the short term, the change in designation would help distinguish Ole Miss journalism as a multi-functional activity encompassing strong teaching, wide-ranging research (including exemplary

104

professional practice by some faculty) and an extensive service mission with major outreach to K-12 education and to the print and broadcast media of our region and beyond. The discipline's extensive alumni relations require considerable administrative attention given large numbers of Ole Miss Journalism alumni in the mass media who are important to   us for their moral and material support. In the longer term, school status would assist the unit in securing additional resources from the state as well as from off-campus donors (e.g., alumni, foundations and news organizations) to better serve its many constituencies. [124]

The proposal did not survive the economic and other pressures facing Ole Miss at that moment. In time, there would indeed be a School of Journalism, a school far grander than Stuart Bullion could have envisioned. But he would not live to see it.

2002: Newswatch: Anchors Hope Walker and Martin Bartlett.

Late in 2003, Bullion was diagnosed with liver cancer, and soon after that he was hospitalized. Once again, leadership of the department passed to Samir Husni, a friend as well as a colleague. Husni visited Bullion virtually every day, keeping him informed of developments back in Farley Hall. Others visited him, too, notably Sherwood Harris, a fellow Princeton alumnus, as well as Bullion's family and many friends and students and faculty. But the cancer was overwhelming. "For the second time in my life," he wrote to a friend, "I have been drafted. I am weak and tired, but my mental energy remains high. . ." Indeed, he took phone calls and sent e-mails from his hospital bed right up to the end.

"He didn't know how to give up," wrote Ronnie Agnew, editor of the state's largest newspaper, the Jackson *Clarion-Ledger*. "He would not let us feel sorry for him. That's because he never felt sorry for himself. He simply prepared himself for battle—and he fought."[125]

On Wednesday, April 21, he died. He was 56.

The printed program for the memorial service before an overflow crowd at the Paris Yates chapel service carried some of Bullion's quotes that had been provided by his students. One of them reflected a favorite saying of his: "Win like you're used to it. Lose like it doesn't matter." To a great many at Ole Miss and beyond, however, the loss of Stuart Bullion, the chairman who cared, mattered a very great deal.

Samir Husni

Mr. Magazine

Samir Husni, chair, Department of Journalism, 1996-97 and 2004-09.

For Samir Husni, a moment that would define his life and career came early, and in an unlikely way. He was eight years old, a pupil in an elementary school in Tripoli, Lebanon, when he got his first comic book. It was an issue of *Superman*, its text in Arabic. He loved what he saw. Comic books have long appealed to kids. But to young Samir Husni, the appeal took a different form. While his friends were captivated by Superman's strength and his derring-do, young Samir was less interested in the story; instead, he was mesmerized by what he could envision to be the sheer power of combining text and graphics with paper and ink. The possibilities were endless, and, on the spot, young Samir was hooked.

In the years that followed, he used his meager allowance money to buy more comic books, then magazines. A fascination became a hobby, a hobby became a fixation, and that fixation, plus his intellect and boundless energy, transformed him into an internationally acclaimed authority. He has been called "the leading magazine expert in this country."[126]

That accolade did not come easily or quickly. First, he earned a bachelor's degree at the University of Lebanon, performing well enough to be admitted to a graduate school in the United States. The university accepting him was North Texas State (later renamed the University of North Texas) which then, as now, boasted a solid program in journalism. Travel and immigration difficulties delayed his arrival in Texas until almost a week after classes had begun. He went to see his major professor, Reg Westmoreland, who regarded him skeptically. The other graduate students were well into their reading, he said, but if Samir could start on this book—he handed him a hefty volume—then maybe he could begin to catch up. The book was *Time, Inc., the Intimate History of a Publishing Enterprise,*[127] and it described how two young men, Henry Luce and Briton Hadden, transformed an idea into a magazine empire. Eagerly, Samir read it in a weekend and was able to present a report at the first meeting he attended of Prof. Westmoreland's graduate seminar. The professor was impressed, and young Samir was on his way.

North Texas gave Samir the opportunity and the methodologies to do serious studies of the mass media. For his master's degree thesis, he wrote a content analysis comparing press coverage by *The Times of London* and *The New York Times* of the Lebanese War of 1975-76. This performance, plus glowing recommendations from his professors at North Texas, got him admitted to the doctoral program at the University of Missouri, the oldest School of Journalism in the world, certainly one of the most respected.

Doctoral students at Missouri were largely free to pursue any research topic, provided they could get their advisory committee to approve of it, and this gave Samir the green light to delve more deeply into the magazine industry that had so long captivated him. Then, as before and since, magazines were in a constant state of change. New titles came and went, and Samir was especially fascinated by the startups, those attempting to attract and hold readers in a hotly competitive media environment. Why had some beginning magazines failed while others succeeded? Endlessly searching the newsstands and the libraries for new titles, Samir found enough of them to justify his doctoral dissertation: *Success and Failure of New Consumer Magazines in the United States, 1979-1983.* That same year, 1983, he was awarded his Ph.D. and prepared to launch a career in teaching and research. And to continue his fascination—his wife called it his obsession—with magazines.

2006: Husni with his magazine class in Italy: Kasimu Harris, Polly Allen, Ashleigh O'Quinn, Daniel Madison, Kilgore Drake, Bishop Porter, Catherine Robinson, Nia Triantis Gillespie.

About that time, and fortunately for all concerned, the Department of Journalism at the University of Mississippi had just decided to launch a modest program in magazine journalism. James Autry, then president of the magazine division at Meredith Corp. publishers of *Better Homes & Gardens* and an enthusiastic alumnus of Ole Miss, was continuously developing and refining his views on magazine presentation. He called what he was doing "Service Journalism," and to Jim Autry that meant not only telling the reader about a subject, but also providing helpful sidebar information for readers who wanted to go visit it or simply to know more. An article about, say, San Francisco should also include information as to how best to get there, where to stay, where to dine, special sights to see, cost information. Now a commonplace practice throughout the media, Jim Autry's idea was new in the early 1970s and 80s. He thought service journalism could become an important part of magazine editorial content, and a university's journalism program would do well to make its students aware of it. Autry persuaded Meredith Corp. to provide some incentive funding for teaching service journalism to an institution of higher learning that might be interested. Dr. Will Norton, then journalism chairman at Ole Miss, jumped at the idea and began telephoning his administrative counterparts, searching for someone to establish and run a program in magazines and service journalism. He could not find the kind of candidate he needed. Then Ken McDougall, director of community relations at the Meredith Corporation, told Dr. Norton about a doctoral candidate from Lebanon "who knows more about American magazines than anybody we've ever seen."[128] It was what Dr. Norton wanted to hear, and that autumn Dr. Samir Husni came on board as an assistant professor of journalism at the University of Mississippi.

It was from this unlikely location—and Oxford, Mississippi, is not exactly thought of as the center of the media universe—that Dr. Husni began to build a reputation that would become global in its scope and influence.

2008: Panel in Farley Hall during the Presidential Debate Week at Ole Miss left to right) Dr. Samir Husni, chair and professor of journalism; Joanne Lipman, editor in chief, Condé Nast *Portfolio Magazine*; Dan Goodgame, managing editor, *Fortune Small Business*; UM's William F. Shughart II, F.A.P. Barnard Distinguished Professor of Economics and editor in chief, *Public Choice*; as well as Bill Rayburn, chief executive officer, FNC. (Photo by Robert Jordan)

As Samir stepped up his relentless research, especially into startup magazines, Jim Autry persuaded the Meredith Corporation in Des Moines to publish Husni's compilation of new entries in the field. The first edition appeared in 1986 and, with Autry's blessing, it was entitled *Samir Husni's Guide to New Magazines*. Some 234 new titles were listed and described, and the publication became a hot discussion topic throughout the magazine industry. The *Husni Guide* became an annual event, even more comprehensive and authoritative as the years wore on. In 2009, as an example, some 704 new consumer magazines were described.[129]

As the *Husni Guide* gained more popularity, publishers and would-be publishers of magazines began to call upon this Ole Miss professor for advice. In an era of fragmented audiences and specialized publications, how does one magazine find—and hold—its niche? Thus was launched a wide-ranging, and lucrative, consulting service that would take Samir Husni over much of the world. His expertise gave him credibility in such critical areas as basic magazine concepts, market positioning, audience analysis, competition analysis, advertising and circulation issues, budgeting, editorial presentation and graphic design.

Beyond that, he was quoted extensively in the magazine trade press. The editor of *Folio*, the magazine industry's leading trade journal, put it this way: "His (Husni's) influence is that it gets out there . . . in the popular press, and people read things they normally wouldn't read about the industry."[130] This vibrant interaction with the mass media also enhanced his teaching. Students appreciated his "real world" associations and the way his ongoing research kept his classes lively and on the leading edge of industry developments.

There was a problem, however, with one student. "He couldn't manage to pronounce my name," Dr. Husni recalls. "He couldn't quite say 'Samir' and he couldn't quite say 'Husni.' So he just referred to me as 'Mr. Magazine.'"

The name stuck, and Husni was delighted. "I love seeing my name in print," he said. "I never tire of it." The license plate on his car is "Mr. Mag." "I am thrilled by this," Husni says, smiling. "I have become a brand."

Sunday Morning correspondent Rita Braver interviews Samir Husni for a segment on the decline in circulation of newspapers. Braver and the CBS *Sunday Morning* crew came to Oxford to tape the segment that aired on March 11, 2007.

As his fame spread far and wide, he began to receive offers from other institutions, some of them located in huge media centers. (From Northwestern University, in Evanston, Ill., from University of Kansas in Lawrence, Kan., as examples.) But by now Ole Miss was in his blood, and he had no desire to leave.

Too, he knew Ole Miss needed him, not "merely" as a nationally prominent expert in his field, but, on occasion, as an administrator. Three times—1990-91, 1994-96, 2004-09—the department chairman's job was vacant, and Dr. Samir Husni was tapped by the central administration to take over the job on an acting or interim basis. By now he was well established on the Ole Miss campus and in the Oxford community, and the chancellor and provost turned to Dr. Husni as a reliable leader fully capable of keeping things running while national searches were underway to find a permanent department chairman. In 2005 Dr. Husni was slected chair of the department on a permanent basis, after a national search for the position. He held the chair's job until the department morphed to a school in 2009.

Dr. Husni's stewardship during these periods proved to be quite successful. And, perhaps more important to him, his hard work and focus ensured that his research in the magazine field did not suffer as a result.

The combination of paper and ink, graphics and text that so fascinated

Samir Husni as a child shows no sign of waning. His home and office overflow with magazines. In 2002 he estimated he had at least 20,000 first editions—that he knew about. Hundreds, perhaps several thousand, more have been added since. Each week he drives to the nearest big city, Memphis, to search the newsstands for new titles. He spends hundreds of dollars each year buying new magazines. And by now, the *Husni Guide* is so well established that many publishers of startup magazines automatically send him their first editions for inclusion in the book.

"The thing so extraordinary about Samir Husni," said the late Donald E. Welsh, former publisher of *Budget Living*, "is that he really is an encyclopedia of the magazine industry. It's amazing how many startups, so many regional magazines no one's heard of, that he includes in his book."[131]

The *Chicago Tribune* described him as "the planet's leading expert on new magazines," while a CBS News report called him "a world renowned expert on print journalism."[132]   He has been interviewed on many television networks, National Public Radio and a host of other radio programs and has been asked to judge national and regional competitions to honor excellence in magazine presentation. In every interview he is identified, at his insistence, as a journalism professor at the University of Mississippi.[133]

His enthusiasm for magazines, unabated so many years after that first look at a comic book, is almost reverential. In his blog, he wrote:

> Magazines are much more than content. Magazines are much more than information, words, pictures and colors all combined in a platform that serves nothing but as a delivery vehicle. Magazines, each and every one and each and every issue of every one, are a total experience that engages the con-sumer's five senses. Nothing is left to chance. It is a total package…. Every issue is a complete new experience with a sense of ownership, showmanship and membership and is renewed with the arrival of the next issue….[134]

Dr. Husni dismisses predictions that the magazine field is out of date and will eventually die out: "In 1985 we had 2,500 consumer magazines and in 2010 we had 10,000. Show me any other 'dying' industry that has given so much birth!" The current American publishing model may be floundering, he adds, but print is not.[135]

Digital technology has provided a variety of new platforms for the presentation of news and information and entertainment. The technological changes prompted Dr. Husni to create a research arm, the Magazine Innovation Center, to help editors adjust to the present and prepare for the years ahead. His *Husni's Guide* now lists book-a-zines and annual magazine startups. "To me," he says, "anything that reaches the general public or the newsstand qualifies."[136] The future, in other words, is not something for journalists to fear.

Dr. Husni has assumed multiple roles during his tenure at Ole Miss. Whenever a chairman left, or resigned, or died, Dr. Husni was asked to take charge. In all, 11 of nearly 30 years he's been at Ole Miss he has been "acting" or "interim" chairman, or simply "chairman." "For years, the title "acting" was a fixture on my business cards," he says. "Even the years I was the permanent chair, it still felt as if it was a transition to something else."[137]

He was asked to lead the program after Will Norton became dean at Nebraska, again after Don Sneed's abrupt resignation and yet again after the death of Stuart Bullion. Despite having to manage with the "interim" or "acting" title, Dr. Husni achieved a very great deal. Such as:

- Leading the Department to full re-accreditation during an especially difficult period. "We were nomads on campus," he recalls, "while our building was being remodeled. Our chair (Dr. Bullion) had died a year earlier, and the morale and status of the faculty hit a prime time low."

- Organizing the rededication ceremony for the reopening of Farley Hall after two years of renovations and additions to the building.

- Creating the Stuart Bullion memorial lecture, and bringing in some of the industry's leading figures to deliver it.

- Navigating the troubled waters -- bureaucratic hassles and soothing faculty apprehensions -- that led the department into its new status as the Ed and Becky Meek School of Journalism and New Media. Although the transition was difficult, with all it entailed in terms of increasing responsibilities and higher expectations, it was nevertheless carried out with relative calm and efficiency.

- Gently nudging the program back from a more bookish orientation, where it had evolved under Stuart Bullion, to one that was more professional.

- And, most of all, being a reliable, steadying influence.

"You have provided strong leadership in troubled times," wrote dean Glenn Hopkins of the College of Liberal Arts. "Thank you for all you have done for Journalism and the College."[138]

By 2011 Dr. Husni was well into his fifties. His hair was thinner, but what remained, like his ever-present moustache, was black and with no traces of gray. The sustained hard work (teaching, relentless research, consulting, administration, prodigious international travel) seemed not to have affected his cheerful disposition or his ability to smile. Officially, he was a full professor and Hederman Lecturer in Journalism and director of the Magazine Innovation Center in the Meek School. Unofficially, to his students and to a wide range of editors and publishers throughout the globe, he was simply "Mr. Magazine."

The Mississippi Scholastic Press Association

Reaching 'em Early

Even before he arrived at the University of Mississippi to create and launch that institution's journalism department, Dr. Charles Gerald Forbes knew he would need to recruit students, good students, into the program. A most effective way to do that was to make sure the kids in high school knew that journalism is an attractive career field, and that Ole Miss would be a good place to prepare for it. He had told the chancellor as much when he was being interviewed for the chairmanship. Asked what he hoped to accomplish, should he be offered the chance to lead the new department, Forbes made out a list of his priorities, and the first item on it was to create some kind of program for the high school boys and girls who worked on their school newspapers.

"Frankly," he would write later, "(I wanted to) get some bright students to thinking about Ole Miss and visiting it. The brightest students in high school generally include those who put out the school paper. It worked for me."[139]

Yes it did. Forbes got the position, and the Mississippi Scholastic Press Association was born. That was in 1947. The original name was The University of Mississippi Press Institute, and its first two-day conference, May 9-10, 1947, attracted 139 students and faculty, representing seven colleges and 18 high schools. The association had hit the ground running.

Forbes pushed hard, realizing that both students and their sponsors would be happy "to take something back home that they could get into their hometown newspapers." So, "I dreamed up some honors and elections that they might put in their local papers when they returned. . . It worked like a charm. The trick was to have enough of these honors for almost every teacher to go home saying 'Look what I did!' The students could likewise boast "See what I did!"

Early on, Forbes got a letter from a teacher, who asked what good was the organization for her? Forbes replied, "I honestly did not know that it was of any value to her, but if I were she I would use it to stimulate my own students, right there in my own classroom." The woman liked the suggestion, Forbes added, and became a booster.[140]

Forbes's prediction, that reaching high school students would pay dividends later, proved correct. He was fond of identifying Ole Miss journalism students who had been attracted to the campus through workshops and conferences put on by the Mississippi Scholastic Press Association.[141]

During the nine years he headed it, the Department of Journalism had only two full-time faculty members. For all his shrewdness and abilities as a salesman, and despite the endless hours he invested in scholastic journalism, Forbes kept himself in the background. Behind the scenes he orchestrated many small-group meetings, arranged for outside professionals as guest speakers and planned dances and other social events for the students.

The organization that Forbes had created—in 1955 the name was changed to the Mississippi Scholastic Press Association—lived on after he left Ole Miss in 1956. Attendance at the spring conferences rose rapidly, and peaked at 701 in 1975. High school teaching efforts, the competitions and the critiques of scholastic papers all got better with each passing year. However, across the country scholastic journalism was taking some hits.

Along with some other extra-curricular activities, the school newspaper and the yearbook sustained budget cuts. More serious was the threat of censorship by ultra-careful school principals, who often intimidated the publications advisers into keeping the school newspaper as bland and free of controversy as possible.

Ultimately this was challenged, and the Supreme Court of the United States sided with student press freedom. In 1969, the court held that students were free to express their opinions—so long as those expressions did not undermine discipline in the school or collide with the rights of others. "It can hardly be argued," the opinion read, "that students abandon their First Amendment rights at the schoolhouse gate."[142] But the promise of this decision was not fully realized, and heavy-handed censorship remained all too prevalent. Particularly galling was the fact that few professional newspapers felt obliged to defend press freedom in their local schools. In 1976, two Ole Miss journalism professors wrote an article for the *Bulletin of the American Society of Newspaper Editors*, entitling it "High School Journalists Are Worth Taking Seriously." It began this way:

ITEM: Newspaper readership, especially among younger adults, is down.

ITEM: High school journalism, for the most part, is in a mess. There is a correlation here, perhaps a profound one. Like most people, high school students tend to think of an institution in terms of their own association with it— and the association most of them have with their own school newspaper probably is not an enthusiastic one. Typically, the adolescent sees his school newspaper paralyzed by heavy-handed censorship, inadequately supported in terms of budget and facilities and advised by an overworked English teacher whose journalistic qualifications, and journalistic interests, probably are minimal.

In short, the teenaged years when so many attitudes are being formed are precisely the years when high school kids are watching their school newspaper being kicked in the face. The impression these young people get here—that journalism isn't worth taking seriously—is likely to endure.

Incredibly, most newspaper editors seem to accept repression of high school publications as a matter of course. Often there is even an editorial nod of approval at a local high school principal who runs a tight ship where controlling the student newspaper is concerned. Only on rare occasions do we hear of the local newspaper coming to the defense of an embattled high school editor.....[143]

Many years later, a certain amount of scholastic press censorship remains. Most often, it takes the form of indirect, or even direct, pressure put on the teacher who, among much else, advises the school newspaper.

When Dr. Gerald Forbes resigned in 1956, he was succeeded by his (only) faculty colleague, Dr. Samuel Talbert. "Dr. Sam" was as keenly interested in MSPA as Dr. Forbes had been, and during the next 16 years the organization grew rapidly—indeed, it became known as one of the best scholastic organizations of its kind in the country.[144] The MSPA had become large enough, and complex enough, for Talbert to shift responsibilities for running to a newly hired faculty member, Prof. S. Gale Denley, who also published his family's weekly newspaper at nearby Bruce. Well known throughout Mississippi, Denley was able to promote the organization's activities as well as to cultivate associations with high school publications advisers and their bosses, the principals. MSPA's services now included summer workshops for newspaper and yearbook staffs and their advisers; a tabloid newspaper, *The Journalist*, with news and advice for improving student publication quality; and more contests and awards. In addition, they established The Silver Em award, which honors outstanding journalists, and the Golden Em, to recognize professors who had been especially helpful to MSPA. The first Golden Em went to "Dr. Sam," and was presented posthumously in his memory.[145]

During the 1970s MSPA's growth was stifled somewhat by an on-campus turf battle with the university's Division of Continuing Education, which demanded control over finances and MSPA's outreach policies. Continuing Education summarily raised the fees charged by MSPA for conferences and workshops—which could affect attendance. Continuing Education also charged "overhead" for overseeing MSPA, a further drain on MSPA's modest treasury. Despite the bureaucratic wrangling, however, MSPA managed to progress. While Prof. Denley remained as head of MSPA, the actual day-to-day work was done by a coordinator, usually a graduate student. In 1977, Dr. Will Norton, by now chairman of the department, was able to establish the coordinator as a regular position. The first coordinator was Susan Langdon, then a graduate student. The resulting improvement in MSPA services was enough to upgrade the MSPA position in 1982 from staff to faculty status. As Susan Langdon stepped aside,[146] Mark Barden took over as the next coordinator. Rosie Eberle, who taught two classes and spent the remainder of her time with MSPA, was his successor. Robin Street, also an instructor, was another coordinator.

A high point came in March, 1984, when the man who started it all, Dr. Gerald Forbes, came back to attend the 35th annual meeting of the scholastic press group he had started. This was his first return to the campus in the 27 years since he had left it. For Dr. Forbes, then 83, the reunion was a joyous one.

"It was wonderful in Temporary A," he said of the Army surplus building that had been the first home of the Department of Journalism back in 1946. "There was such camaraderie among the students. The kids all were interested in the same thing and they could get acquainted with each other over there." [147]

Dr. Forbes was justifiably gratified at the growth of the Mississippi Scholastic Press Association. He could not have known, however, that its best days were ahead.

First advisory board for MSPA, 2005-2012 (left to right): Sherry McKenzie, Tupelo High school; Leona O'Neal, George County High School; Beth Fitts, MSPA, executive director; and Lou Callum, Madison Central High School.

120

The MSPA's great leap forward accelerated in 2003 when Elizabeth L. Fitts took over as director. Already acclaimed as an outstanding publications adviser, Beth Fitts brought great energy and resourcefulness to MSPA, making it one of the most effective, and certainly most active, scholastic press organizations in the nation. Under her leadership, MSPA by 2010 had expanded its operations to include:

- Technology workshops, including podcasting, latest broadcasting and desktop publishing techniques, and digital photography

- Publication critiques, including mail-in and on-site critique services.

- Summer camps, including "Advisor Bootcamp" as well as camps for newspaper and yearbook student staffs.

- Credits and lab training for advisers

- Workshops targeting different areas of the state

- Journalistic basics in specialized areas, such as interviewing, news reporting and editing, publication design, advertising, photography, PhotoShop, and feature writing.

- Spring conventions attracted about 500 students and faculty advisers who were offered 70 classes in newspaper, yearbook, magazine, on-line communication, broadcast and social media.

"She's maybe the best in the business," said Dr. Bruce Konkle, who directed the highly regarded South Carolina Scholastic Press Association. "I don't know anybody in our field better liked or more respected than Beth Fitts." [148]

Others share that view. In her distinguished career, Beth Fitts has earned many honors, including:

- Dow Jones National High School Journalism Teacher of the Year (2003)

- *USA Today* All-Star Teacher Team (2001)

- National Scholastic Press Association Pioneer Award (2008)

- Distinguished Service Award, Southern Interscholastic Press

Association (2005)

- Mississippi Newspaper Adviser of the Year (five times)

- Oxford School District Teacher of the Year (2002, 2003)

- Guest faculty at scholastic press associations and other states, and author of articles in various professional and scholastic journals

A smiling, yet serene woman with deep religious convictions, Beth Fitts has taken the Meek School at Ole Miss to the very top in a most important field. MSPA has been successful far beyond what the man who started it all, Dr. Gerald Forbes, could have envisioned. He would have been very proud. In 2013 she retired, and R. J. Morgan was named an instructor and director of MSPA.

Student Media

Getting the Words Right

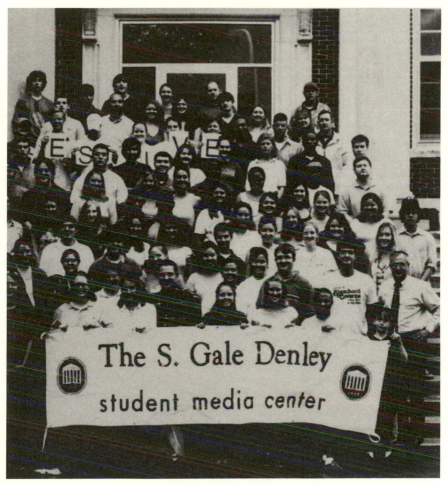

2004: Student Media Center staff

PRINT

There are bigger campus newspapers than *The Mississippian*, and some may be slicker, in terms of graphic design. But few, if any, student newspapers have been read as extensively by their state's political leaders, and few if any have endured more criticism and clamors for censorship. And few, if any, student newspapers have been defended more vigorously by their central administrations than *The Mississippian*. "*The Mississippian* is the conscience of Ole Miss," said a former dean in the Office of Student Affairs, Sparky Reardon. "It whispers in the ears of the Lyceum."[149] If *The Mississippian* can sometimes be a thorn in the side of chancellors and deans, it is also a source of fierce, protective pride.

The Mississippian began in 1911, a merger of two frail publications, the monthly *University of Mississippi Magazine* and a weekly newspaper, the *Varsity Voice,* neither of which could long survive on a campus of fewer than 600 students. *The Mississippian* was something of a social club, written mostly by English majors who felt creative or, perhaps, possessed a mischievous streak. Two enterprising business managers sold enough subscriptions and advertising to keep the paper afloat. The first editor was Forrest G. Moore, and during that year he felt emboldened to editorialize on controversial topics. One such piece so stirred up the campus that mass meetings of protest were held in classes and a special faculty meeting was called to demand his expulsion. The resolution of condemnation was passed, but when it reached the desk of the chancellor, A. A. Kincannon, it simply died there.[150]

Thus began a pattern: (1) *The Mississippian* prints something controversial, followed by (2) demands, sometimes from on campus, sometimes from powerful politicians in Jackson, to censor the paper and/or remove the editor, followed by (3) the chancellor refusing to do either. That pattern would be repeated many times in the century to follow.

Surviving its first year, *The Mississippian* gamely plunged ahead. On page one, just under the nameplate, was the proud—some would call it defiant—declaration that the paper is "Published by Students of the University of Mississippi." That was quite literally the truth. The paper's only financial support came from advertising and subscription sales. The reporters and editors had no office space; they did their work from their dormitory rooms. The business managers somehow brought in the $1,200 a month required to keep *The Mississippian* solvent. The paper was a weekly, usually of eight pages. During World War I, with staff depleted by enlistments and the fragile economy of Oxford forcing merchants to limit their ad buys, the paper sometimes could muster only four pages.

During the 1920s, the paper's finances improved, as did the university's. In 1926, *The Mississippian* rolled out its "Second Coming" banner headline type to proclaim that enrollment at Ole Miss had passed the 1,000 mark. Though generally upbeat, and heavy with sports news, the paper still could be controversial. One editor was beaten up on campus, and another kept a loaded pistol in his desk.

Things got worse during the Great Depression, as enrollment fell off and advertising sales declined. Though sometimes only four pages per issue,

The Mississippian persisted. Later in the 1930s, however, the economy had recovered sufficiently for the paper to observe its birthday in 1937 with a 24-page edition and an impressive gathering of professional journalists on hand for the party.[151]

But later, as war clouds gathered over Europe, *The Mississippian*'s editorial content grew far more serious.

When the war did break out, college papers throughout the nation were hit hard. William Winter was editor of *The Mississippian* in 1942. In one of his last editorials before heading off to become an Army officer, he wrote:

> Word came from State College this week that *The Reflector*, the splendid newspaper of the Maroons, had succumbed to the exigencies of war. The authorities announced that Mississippi State College publications were at an end for the duration. We regret to learn of that, for we had always read with interest the paper of our collegiate neighbors of Oktibbeha.[152]
>
> And the fact that *The Mississippian* is still on its feet does not mean that it is immune to the same problems that put the other publications out of commission. For rather the publication of *The Mississippian* after the current semester is going to be a job that will tax the ingenuity and resourcefulness of whoever has the responsibility of handling the affairs of the editor's and business manager's offices.[153]

Four weeks later Winter was in uniform. Two members of his *Mississippian* staff would be killed in the war, as would three former presidents of the Ole Miss student body. The paper reported news, as best it could, of Ole Miss students in the military. The content was not unlike that of a large family letter, and when members of the Ole Miss community were killed or captured or missing in action, *The Mississippian* carried as many of the grim details as were available. Despite the hardships imposed by the war, *The Mississippian*, according to Winter, emerged stronger than ever. "Much of that was due to the spirited emergence of the Ole Miss women to leadership positions. Maralyn Howell was the first female to be elected ASB president in the spring of 1943, and Miriam Horne and Huldah Cousins became editors of *The Mississippian* the following two years. They led the way to the inspirational role that women have played in the history of Ole Miss since that time."[154]

After the war, returning veterans, and the G.I. Bill for financial support of them, swelled the university's enrollment and prompted the demand for a more diverse curriculum. One manifestation of this growth and change was the creation of a Department of Journalism. This new curriculum was an immediate success, in terms of student popularity. Dr. Gerald Forbes, the department's chairman and only professor, was eager for his students to write articles and to see them in print. The logical publication outlet was *The Mississippian*. Forbes had no interest in controlling *The Mississippian*, and he knew the chancellor was firmly committed to keeping the paper free from any kind of faculty or administrative control. So Forbes simply made available to *The Mississippian* the articles produced by his News Reporting students and the paper's student editors were free to decide, on a story-by-story basis, which pieces to use. Chronically short on copy, and often understaffed, *The Mississippian* editors appreciated the opportunity presented by this rich new infusion of copy.

While other *Mississippian* editors had been known to chide the state's tenaciously conservative culture, in 1950 a kid from Pascagoula blasted it with the editorial version of a hand grenade. His name was Albin J. Krebs, and he committed what many regarded as the unpardonable sin: He called for an end to racial segregation in Mississippi.

Though schools outside the Deep South were gradually integrating, the prevailing law, not yet overturned by the Supreme Court, permitted segregation so long as the institutional facilities were "separate but equal." Krebs argued that since Mississippi had only one state-supported law school, and it was open only to whites, the law was clearly being violated.

That editorial and others in a similar vein that followed set off a firestorm, both on and off the campus. Political leaders, including powerful state officials, demanded that Krebs be expelled. And, they cried, if the chancellor wouldn't do it, then he, too, should be dismissed. The chancellor quietly reminded the legislature and the general public that *The Mississippian* was a student operation, and he had no desire or authority to control it.

Amid the editorial outcries from the legislature and much of the state's press, Ole Miss students, many of them, demonstrated against Krebs. One protest rally outside Krebs's dorm drew a crowd estimated at 2,000 students, where a cross was burned amidst noisy demands that Krebs be disciplined or expelled or worse. Chancellor Williams calmly announced that the protesters, too, had a right to express their opinion, just as did Albin Krebs.[155]

Krebs doubled down on his outspoken editorial position attacking loyalty oaths, smear tactics in anti-communist investigations and other causes that were championed by arch-conservatives in Mississippi and throughout the country. In the face of the protests, Krebs fired back:

> A country becomes a police state when its citizens, be they college professors or ditch diggers, are forced by the state to knuckle under to what a few politicians call 'the proper attitude.'[156]

Krebs never wavered, although—perhaps to take some of the heat off the chancellor—he did make it clear in an editorial that he was not speaking for the university or, for that matter, anyone but himself.

Eventually things quieted down. Mississippi would remain a segregated state for some time, and Krebs finished out his year as editor. His courage and his brilliance would eventually carry him to a distinguished career with *The New York Times*. But his final year at Ole Miss also brought him considerable pain. He was widely denounced and physically threatened by his fellow students. His roommate moved out. When he got his degree, he would not return to the campus for 35 years. "A long time coming," wrote a contemporary, Liz Shiver, "but he did so and left a legacy to the Department of Journalism."[157]

Editors of *The Mississippian* were more than student journalists, they were bigger-than-life campus heroes as well. One of the best of these was Paul Pittmann, later to become a successful publisher and authoritative commentator on Mississippi and national affairs. His successor as editor, Lawrence J. Franck, wrote of Pittmann, "Could he be present here, and could I, I would follow him around as I did when he was editor of *The Mississippian* and I was an apprentice college newspaperman and, for whatever reasons, Paul's protege and his friend. I would laugh at his stories, endure his practical jokes and perform whatever assignments he might give me. For I sat at Paul's feet then and, given the chance, would again."[158]

Of Charles Overby, *Mississippian* editor in the late 1960s, one of his staff members wrote: "I once got into trouble with Charles. I wrote a rather sarcastic piece about one of the fraternities. Even though we were great friends, he let me know he was disappointed with my lack of objectivity. It was a great lesson, though I was crushed to have disappointed him."[159]

In 1961, at age 50, *The Mississippian* broke out of its weekly status. The Publications Board, which exerted nominal fiscal control, and the growing Department of Journalism, along with the chancellor encouraged the shift to a four-times-a-week publication schedule. The paper obtained a used press and moved its editorial and production operations into the ramshackle confines of Brady Hall, placing the paper and the Department under the same roof.

The editor that year was James Robertson, later to become a justice of the Mississippi Supreme Court, and his capable, self-deprecating leadership mitigated the problems posed by the transition. In addition to the quickening pace for news and editorial content, adjustments were required for the ad sales and production and delivery operations. These were overcome, and the *DM*, as it was now referred to on campus, moved gracefully into its new situation. But the paper's biggest confrontation would come the following year.

James Meredith, an African-American Mississippian who had served a hitch in the Air Force, was determined to earn a degree from Ole Miss. Persistently, he fought through bureaucratic denials and delays and lawsuits and, at long last, was grudgingly given permission by the courts to enroll. But those who knew anything about the Meredith case knew that admitting him could bring trouble. The Kennedy White House got involved, and the Department of Justice dispatched dozens of federal marshals and some 3,000 soldiers to the Oxford campus, where demonstrations and riots had already broken out. The night before Meredith's scheduled admission, an ugly situation got worse. Charles W. Eagles, an Ole Miss history professor who wrote the definitive book of the Meredith situation, described the scene this way:

> Meredith's surroundings resembled an "eerie military camp." Riot debris littered the heart of the campus. Soldiers manned all entrances and patrolled the town and campus. MPs guarded Baxter Hall, while marshals rested in and around the Lyceum. A field hospital occupied an athletic field, and the army converted an intramural field into a motor pool. While the student union grill remained closed, the campus cafeteria served meals with paper plates and plastic utensils, but without its black employees, who all stayed away.[160]

JAMES MEREDITH AT OLE MISS – PHOTOGRAPHS BY ED MEEK

Student demonstrators, Ole Miss, Sept. 30, 1962

James Meredith surrounded by media.

In the Circle near the Lyceum on Oct. 1, 1962, the morning after the riot opposing Meredith's enrollment at Ole Miss.

U.S. Army units take up position during occupation of Ole Miss and Oxford.

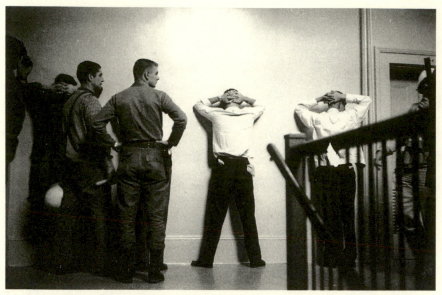

Students detained during the riot over the enrollment of Meredith.

James Meredith is escorted to his first class at Ole Miss
by Chief U.S. Marshal James McShane (left) and John Doar
of the Department of Justice.

James Meredith sits alone in a class that no white students would attend.

Student stands to leave class that Meredith attended.

James Meredith at graduation ceremonies in 1963.

There was bloodshed. A foreign journalist, Paul Leslie Guihard, 30, reporting for the *London Daily Sketch* and for Agence France Presse, died from a .38 caliber bullet in the back. A local resident, Walter Ray Gunter, 23, was killed by a bullet to the head. Gunter's death presumably was caused by a stray bullet. Guihard's was not.[161]

The *Daily Mississippian's* editor, Sidna Brower, courageously stood up to the mob. In an editorial entitled "Violence Will Not Help," she wrote:

> This is an appeal to the entire student body and to anyone concerned with the present situation. Not only do the students chance forfeiting their education by participating in riots, but they are bringing dishonor and shame to the university and to the State of Mississippi.
>
> When students hurled rocks, bottles and eggs, the federal marshals were forced to resort to tear gas to back off the crowds.
>
> Outsiders . . .I beg you to go home.
>
> This is a battle between the State of Mississippi and the United States government; the university is caught in the middle. The Civil War was fought one hundred years ago over almost the same issues and the United States of America prevailed. The federal government is once again showing the strength and power to uphold the laws of our country....
>
> Whatever your beliefs, you are a citizen of the United States of America and of the State of Mississippi, and should preserve peace and harmony of both governments.[162]

Sidna Brower Mitchell

For this and for her ensuing editorials, equally gutsy, Sidna Brower was nominated for the Pulitzer Prize. She was also denounced as "The foul harlot of journalism" by a conservative publication, *Rebel Underground*. And, perhaps most painful to her, formally censured in a resolution adopted by the campus Senate for "failing in a time of grave crisis to represent and uphold the rights of fellow students."

"I certainly found out who my friends and supporters were," she would write later.

She did not win the Pulitzer Prize—to her relief, she said. "Where could I go professionally if I won that distinguished prize as a 21-year-old college student?"

Significantly, she noted "that while the administration kept me apprised of what was happening regarding James Meredith's attempted admission to the university and later when he was enrolled, they never once told me what to write or not write regarding any situation. Later I would receive letters from university officials thanking me for my stand."

The icing on the cake would come much later—some 41 years later, in fact. In 2002 the campus Senate repealed that censure of Sidna Brower and commended her for "the outstanding journalistic courage displayed throughout her tenure as editor of the *Daily Mississippian*."[163]

But if Sidna Brower's editorship prompted a storm of criticism, so, to a lesser degree, did many of the others. James Robertson ('62) was denounced by state political figures as part of "the atheists and communist sympathizers" on the campus." Later Robertson admitted to Otis Tims ('73) that, "Some days I would wake up and think, 'I just don't have the stomach to go through this another day.' But I wanted so badly to show that someone who was 21 could have reasonable thoughts. I remember that it was absolutely imperative to resist stinging folks that really needed to be stung. But that would have been counter-productive."[164]

Jim Autry ignited a controversy, but he reveled in it: "I consider my finest hour to be when a Mississippi state legislator rose to condemn *The Mississippian* and me by name. On the floor of the legislature. Ha."[165]

The denunciation of Autry was prompted by a blistering editorial he wrote in opposition to a new policy, adopted by the Board of Trustees of the Institutions of Higher Learning, which read, in part:

> All speakers invited to the campuses of any of the State Institutions of Higher Learning must first be investigated and approved by the head of the institution involved and when invited the names of such speakers must be filed with the executive secretary of the board of trustees.

To that, Autry had this to say:

> If democracy is what we have been taught to believe, it will be able to withstand the onslaughts of all the opposition.

137

We believe in democracy and we believe the people will do the right thing when properly informed. The only way to be properly informed is to have absolute freedom of thought and discussion.[166]

James A. Autry

Chancellor Williams sent the board a letter objecting to the policy and, in fact, quietly refused to comply with it.

After Williams retired, the new chancellor, Porter Fortune, would fend off comparable pressures. When some students at Mississippi State organized a club for gays and lesbians, the chancellor was told by the board not to permit the *Daily Mississippian* to write anything about it lest a similar group be formed at Ole Miss. Chancellor Fortune ignored the order. In a later action, the board of trustees directed the heads of each Mississippi college or university to appoint a faculty member as official censor of student publications. Laying his own job on the line, Dr. Fortune confronted the board directly, saying he had no intention of allowing an official censor at Ole Miss. The board backed down. For this and other courageous acts, the chancellor was chosen the first winner of the Elijah Parish Lovejoy Award,[167] presented by Ball State University to honor a college or university administrator who had defended student press freedom.

On various occasions, Dr. Fortune would receive late-night phone calls demanding that he forbid the *Daily Mississippian* to print this or that controversial story. When the hour grew late, Dr. Fortune would simply unplug the telephone and go to sleep. He said little about such pressures, but *Mississippian* editors and journalism professors knew the chancellor was taking heat in their behalf.

Between controversies—that is to say, most of the time—the *Daily Mississippian* simply, and routinely, chronicled the day-to-day activities of the university. At the 100th anniversary reunion of *Mississippian* staffers, Charles Overby pointed out that the *DM* somehow captured perfectly the multilayered, quirky spirit of Ole Miss. As an example, he pointed to the front page of the issue of July 6, 1962. The banner headline that day was WILLIAM FAULKNER IS DEAD. The only other multi-column headline on the page was BATON TWIRLING INSTITUTE IS SET.

Overby ('68) would eventually be a Pulitzer prize-winning editor, chief of a division of Gannett Newspapers, and CEO of the Freedom Forum. Jim Autry ('55) would head up a national magazine empire. William Winter ('43) would be one of the great governors in Mississippi history. Jimmy Robertson ('62) went from Ole Miss to Harvard Law School and later was a distinguished judge. Louis Silver ('42) became a top executive at *U. S. News & World Report*. Danny Goodgame ('75) was chosen a Rhodes Scholar and after his time at Oxford made it big with *Time, Inc*. Other editors have been similarly successful.

As have their staff colleagues. "Nothing prepared me more than spending time. . .working on the *Daily Mississippian*," writes Steven J. Diffey ('93). "We (the staff) were very close and we put out a great product." Todd Vineyard ('92) praised "the hands-on experience at the *Daily Mississippian*. . .The experience of working in a newsroom environment was very valuable to me. I was well prepared." Mac Demere ('76) writes "Working on the *Mississippian* was the key to my career. I was able to compare my work to professionals who covered the same events." In that same vein, writes Michael Newsom ('05), "The time I spent as campus news editor and also as a staff writer at the *Daily Mississippian* was about the best preparation I could get for a newspaper job."[168]

Through the years, *The Mississippian* staff has encompassed all types— males and females; whites, African-Americans, Hispanics, Asian-Americans; Greeks and independents; talent from out-of-state and talent home-grown; liberals, conservatives, and those who don't care much one way or the other. There is no common pattern.

But if there could be a unifying philosophical thread, something they all could honor and respect, it was stated by Jim Autry at the 100th anniversary reunion: "Just get the words right."

Glamor and controversy aside, however, there has always been the unrelenting pressure simply to prepare a campus newspaper for publication—all that while carrying a load of classes and, maybe, holding down a part-time job as well. Campus journalists aren't often cut much slack in, say, an economics class, where the professor is unlikely to be unimpressed that one of his students had spent much of the night before putting together a complicated news story for the *DM*. Sidna Brower, for all the notoriety she generated during the James Meredith crisis, still had to make it back to the Kappa house before the 11 p.m. curfew. "We fought less for noble ideals than against a thousand little demons that conspired against us," recalls Otis Tims ('73, one of the ablest of *Daily Mississippian* editors: "classes, mechanical breakdowns, wayward reporters, lost copy."[169]

The technology has changed, but the grind hasn't. Back in 1932 Don Townsend concluded his editorship of *The Mississippian* with this in his weary final editorial:

> "What have you done," the angel asked,
> "That I should admit you here?"
> "I ran a paper," the editor replied,
> "For one of my college years."
>
> The angel pityingly shook his head
> And gravely touched a bell,
> "Come in, poor thing, and accept your harp,
> You've had your time in hell."[170]

Hell it might have seemed at the time. But it was also one hell of a ride, and most of those who got on board wouldn't have missed it.

BROADCAST

Ole Miss got involved with radio, after a fashion, early in the 1920s.[171] Only a few years after Guglielmo Marconi had given the world a glimpse of the possibilities of wireless communication, the Physics and Astronomy Department at Ole Miss began tinkering with the new medium. Interested in radio primarily for experimental and technical and teaching reasons, the physics professors soon found there were programming possibilities too—enough that in 1920 the university asked for, and received, the license for a radio station that would carry regular, if limited, broadcasts. The station was designated 5YE. Not many folks in the area had access to radio receivers, but those who did could get music from the university's band and orchestra and glee club and live reports from some Ole Miss athletic events, along with weather reports and news passed along from other stations. Beyond that, the Physics Department used the station to gather and relay technical information for teaching and research purposes.

Eventually, as federal agencies obtained regulatory authority over the mushrooming radio industry, Ole Miss reorganized 5YE and rechristened the station WCBH. There were at the time 700 licensed radio stations in the country. Combinations of stations, or networks, were being organized and they brought big money (advertising) and better quality programming to their growing audiences. But if WCBH had potential, it also proved expensive, in terms of manpower and equipment, and the cost was more than the Physics Department was willing or able to pay. In 1927, when the WCBH license was up for renewal, Ole Miss simply let the license lapse.[172]

The station would be reborn two decades later, this time with the support of the university's public relations staff, extension service people and the Speech Department. The station was eventually housed in the Continuation Center. Advertising income, largely from big tobacco companies, helped pay the freight. Speech faculty taught such courses as "Radio Speech," described in the catalogue as "The theory and techniques of voice methods suited to radio broadcast; basic preparation in all types of radio programs."[173]

Courses such as this appealed to students, and before long there was a Radio-TV Division within the Department of Speech—three professors and more than a hundred majors, following a curriculum many regarded as soft and suspect. There was talk of merging Radio-TV with the Department of Journalism. However, those in the central administration were not prepared to pony up the funding needed to strengthen Radio-TV, in terms of additional equipment and faculty. As a result Journalism felt it could not absorb the broadcast division without weakening its print program, perhaps to the point that its hard-won accreditation might be endangered. This created a certain amount of frustration within the Department of Journalism, where the faculty was well aware of the importance of broadcast news. Dr. Sam Talbert, back in his day, had called for a sequence in broadcast journalism. But such a sequence, if done right, would eat money, and there wasn't enough in the Journalism budget to begin with.

In the late 1970s, journalism's chair, Will Norton, was told that the Speech faculty's interests had shifted to theater productions and traditional public speaking classes, not Radio-TV, and that Journalism should take over the broadcast sequence. Shrewdly, Norton called in an outside consultant, dean Neale Copple of the University of Nebraska, to analyze the situation. Copple's report, which the central administration found persuasive, outlined how Broadcast Journalism could fit into the existing framework, and explained the additional funding necessary to make it succeed. When in 1979, the university agreed, Norton and the Journalism colleagues were pleased. "We don't know much about broadcasting," Norton said, "but we do know news."

It took a while, but the new faculty, new equipment, and a substantially beefed-up broadcast news curriculum, transformed the old Radio-TV sequence into a solid professional program, one that received full national accreditation. The union of print and broadcast, long overdue, finally got done, and done right.

Strong new faculty provided Broadcast News the gravitas it needed. Jim Pratt was a leader as well as an excellent teacher and his sense of professionalism infused his students. He came to Ole Miss with years of experience—he had been a news director at two different stations in Texas—and he had an earned doctorate in communications from the University of Texas. This combination of professional and academic credentials empowered him, and his Broadcast News sequence at Ole Miss, with instant credibility. Before his arrival, the program lacked a sense of direction; Pratt gave it one, and did much to reconcile various approaches and egos among the faculty. There wasn't yet enough equipment, much less a clear policy as to how that equipment should be used most effectively. Pratt was able to get the best out of what there was.[174]

Pratt's objectives were to:

- Pursue a commercial radio station.
- Develop a daily cable television news program.
- Strengthen the quality of broadcast news instruction.
- Place Ole Miss broadcast news graduates in some of the best jobs in the nation.

"Jim Pratt was someone on whom I always could count," Will Norton wrote, after Pratt's death in 2003. "He was someone who always told me the truth, even when it was painful. He was an exceptional broadcaster, a professional who, during his tenure, enabled the Department of Journalism to produce some of the best young broadcasters in America." [175]

Another superb hire was Ralph Braseth. "On my first day of college, Ralph Braseth was assigned as my academic adviser," recalls Andrew Abernathy ('08). "He sat me down and said 'Andrew, I am a mediocre journalism professor but you're lucky because I am the best damned adviser on this campus.'... I remember thinking this place has a sense of humor and wants to invest time in me... I suddenly wanted to learn more."[176]

Television, of the closed circuit variety, became a working news lab and by the early '80s Channel 12, or "Tel-O-Miss News," evolved into well-produced newscast, and in 1984 it began airing nightly on local cable. Amy Carlisle DeLuca ('90) is grateful for "having to produce stories on a daily basis for live newscasts on campus, starting with a morning news meeting, editing up until the last minute and making it on the air, just like 'the real thing.' Having a genuine resumé tape upon graduation was a tremendous advantage and resulted in three job offers right out of college."[177]

Travis Llewellyn ('05) recalls, "The Student Media Center was fantastic for me as an undergrad. I was very involved with Newswatch 12 and Rebel Radio. These activities served me well in my endeavors as a professional. The teachers were fantastic. I was very lucky to have such caring people lead our classes."[178]

When Llewellyn wrote this, he had become Director of Multimedia/New Media for the Sun Belt Conference. The Student Media Center at Ole Miss opened up to him the opportunity to work with newspaper, magazine, radio, television and on-line outlets at once. This built-in diversity of platforms, with new as well as "old" media, respects the concept Ed Meek envisioned when he enriched the school that bears his name.

MAGAZINES

Much the oldest of the student media at Ole Miss is the magazine. Indeed, one university historian, Dr. David Sansing, asserts that student-produced magazines did much to establish Ole Miss traditions and to shape the university's identity.[179] Founded in 1856, the student magazine in 1895 changed its name from *Mississippi University Magazine* to the *University of Mississippi Magazine*. The year before, the editor had bawled out his fellow students for not buying subscriptions. "If you are not patriotic enough to subscribe to it you are unfit to be a student at a great university like this," he wrote. "You had better be home picking cotton." He went on to predict that "anyone who would not pay $1.00 for his own college magazine will never amount to much."[180]

In the years that followed, magazines came and went, published in various formats and under various names. The Department of Journalism made a stab at magazine publishing in 1961. The chairman, Dr. Samuel Talbert, wanted his students to get some practice in writing for a specific audience, and in magazine layout and design. Little funding support was available, and the Department's magazine didn't last long. In 1975, Dr. Will Norton revived it, and saw the publication honored for two consecutive years as the best in the four-state region by the Society of Professional Journalists. That success did much to persuade James A. Autry, an alumnus who by now headed the vast magazine division of the Meredith Corporation to get from his company funding to support a Magazine Sequence within the Department of Journalism at Ole Miss.

For a while, *The Ole Miss Magazine*, as it was now called, had for its faculty adviser Willie Morris, one of the brightest lights in American journalism and literature. A native Mississippian, Morris had earned a degree

143

from the University of Texas. In the process he demonstrated such promise as to win him a Rhodes Scholarship. Upon his return from England, he was one of the founders of *The Texas Observer*, a liberal magazine with a national audience, and eventually he joined the staff of *Harper's* magazine in New York. Four years later he was named editor—the youngest person ever to head so influential a literary magazine. In that capacity he helped nurture the careers of William Styron and Norman Mailer, among other literary giants.[181]

Years later, he yearned to return to his roots in Mississippi, and was hired as writer-in-residence at Ole Miss. He authored more books, significant ones, taught some classes in journalism, advised the student magazine, and even, on occasion, wrote for it. One of his pieces was "Pete and Frances," a revealing glimpse at the deep affection he had developed for life on Faculty Row at Ole Miss. "Pete" was the big, black Labrador retriever he had brought with him from Long Island. "Frances" was a neighbor. The piece ended this way:

> The other day, I was sitting at my work table doing nothing. In my driftless malaise I glanced out my window. There they were, Frances and Pete, silhouetted in an autumn's twilight high on Faculty Row, a lovely human being and a lovely animal there in the lustrous gloaming. Caught then in that affectionate frieze, deep as time, they made me feel, with a twinge of sad happiness, that old mortality on this earth is sometimes not as bad as it could be.[182]

In 2011, fortified by support from the Meek endowment, the Ed and Becky Meek School of Journalism and New Media brought out another magazine, a worthy successor to the award-winning Delta Project of the previous year. This was a 120-page magazine devoted entirely to a depth report on the city of Greenville. The student-produced content, bittersweet prose and poignant art and photographs, was a chronicle of Greenville, a city which had seen better days. The lead article began this way:

> For one brief shining moment, Greenville thought it might just be Mississippi's Camelot.
> It was the "Queen City of the Delta," a regional powerhouse, a busy Mississippi River port, a place with the Delta's only shopping malls, home to a Pulitzer Prize-winning newspaper and the longtime chairman of the Mississippi Republican Party.
> Through the 1950s, '60s and '70s, it looked like Greenville couldn't lose. It was the "Towboat Capital of the World," base to a home-grown shipbuilding and barge industry that employed thousands. When the rest of the Delta was trying to

seduce small sewing plants that employed dozens, Greenville had manufacturing plants that hired hundreds. It landed plants from the likes of Boeing and Vlasic. It had a Schwinn bicycle factory, Chicago Mills and a branch of one of the largest carpet companies in the nation....

Greenville was home to a thriving cultural scene and a stable of nationally known authors. The city integrated its schools peacefully, hired black policemen and employed black store clerks before much of the rest of the state, building a reputation as one of the most progressive places in Mississippi. Stokely Carmichael famously called it "the rest stop for the civil rights movement."

And then it all went away. Camelot turned out to be a myth. Greenville had been living on borrowed time. Its large population of poor people, its *de facto* segregated schools and its fragile, vulnerable economic base caught up with it, a trend all across the Delta. In that respect, the city turned out to be no different after all.

Today, Greenvillians shake their heads at the town's fall and longingly recall when stores were packed on Washington Avenue, when Greenville "was a place so proud of itself it strutted sitting down," as Hodding Carter III, former editor and owner of the *Delta Democrat-Times*, says . . .[183]

The magazine was entitled *Whatever Happened to Main Street?* and it produced a thoughtful, detailed analysis of an important Mississippi city. The articles were honest and thorough, gritty yet not without hope that a heavy dose of harsh reality can somehow be reversed. Powerful and informative, *Whatever Happened to Main Street?* is student journalism, professional journalism, for that matter, at the top of its game, shining light on an important situation, doing what the Founding Fathers must have sensed could be done when they adopted the First Amendment to the Constitution.[184]

Ed Meek

The Benefactor

Ed Meek

Horatio Alger never met Ed Meek. If he had, that famous author of the rags-to-riches novels that inspired the nation more than a century ago would likely have written the Ed Meek story.

Ed Meek didn't begin in rags, but his family's modest, conflicted situation would start him pretty far down in the pack. As a boy in the small Mississippi town of Charleston, he would often sleep under the house to get away from the polar opposites who were his parents: His father was an electrician and plumber who drank too much. His mother was a pillar of the Baptist church. There was little money. The only opportunities open to Ed Meek would be those he could somehow create for himself.

As it turned out, he created a great many of them, developing successful businesses that made him a millionaire many times over. He received the highest honor his state could bestow. He lived to see a proud school of journalism—a program he loved at a university he loved—named for him and for his wife, the childhood sweetheart he had married half a century earlier.

His story is all the more remarkable because he earned his fortune through resourcefulness and hard work, and without running roughshod over other people as he worked his way up. "I've known Ed Meek for 50 years,"

147

remarked a close friend, "and I have never, ever heard him say anything bad about anybody."[185]   Leo Durocher, the fiery baseball manager, famously remarked that "nice guys finish last." Like Horatio Alger, Leo Durocher never met Ed Meek either.

Edwin Ernest Meek was born in Hinds County, near Jackson, Mississippi, but moved very early to Oakland, then, in 1950, to Charleston, a tiny farming community in Delta country.[186]   By his own admission, he was indifferent to his studies but he showed up in church on Sundays (his mother's influence). He was awarded a medal for 12 years of perfect attendance at Sunday School.

When he was a sixth grader, two developments changed his life and defined his future.

One was an after-school job with the *Mississippi Sun*, a weekly serving Tallahatchie County. The publishers, Bill and Jean May, used him as a printer's devil/apprentice assigned to handle chores ranging from hand-setting type to running errands. During the summers, the job became full-time. Meek says his salary remained constant, $7.35 a week. (His publisher claims Meek was overpaid.) But Bill and Jean May taught Meek a great deal about newspaper work, and the three of them would remain lifelong friends. Largely because of this experience, Meek in his senior year was elected editor of the *Black and Gold*, the East Tallahatchie High newspaper, and voted into the school's Hall of Fame. The seed planted in the back shop of the *Mississippi Sun* had taken root. Ed Meek would be involved with journalism the rest of his life

The other development, also occurring during his sixth grade, came when Ed Meek understood that if he worked hard, and worked smart, he could make money. For a start, he mowed lawns. He used a push mower at first, and with it cut enough yards to enable him to buy a gas-powered model for the next summer. The new mower increased his business substantially.

Not until his final semester of his high school senior year did he dare think about going to college. His English teacher, a Mrs. Dan Frederic, graded on what she called a "contract system" whereby a student could set a goal and aspire to reach it. A grade of C required little effort, and Ed initially opted for this track. But as the semester wore on, Ed noticed some of his classmates shooting for a grade of A, which required writing a term paper. After initially regarding this as impossible—then later feeling he somehow was a slacker—he gritted his teeth and made the decision to write a term paper. He got his A.

Toward the end of his senior year, Mrs. Frederic, who was impressed with the work Ed could do once he put his mind to it, told him he should think about going to college. This seemed out of the question. Ed's overall academic record was undistinguished. More to the point, he didn't have nearly enough money. (Though he had managed, through his lawn mowing enterprise, to loan his older brother John $125 to begin his studies at Mississippi State.)[187] After the talk with Mrs. Frederic, Ed brought up the subject of college with his mother. She encouraged him to go for it, but they both knew he

148

would somehow be on his own to come up with the money. Ed spoke to his Congressman, Jamie Whitten, about a summer job with the Forest Service in Montana. Other young men from Mississippi had been selected for that high-paying work as firefighters. There was a minimum age requirement of 18, and Ed was only 17. But Whitten, a wily politician who represented that district for more than a quarter of a century, advised Ed simply not to mention the age thing. He went to Montana, spent the summer battling forest fires, earning good money and having little opportunity to spend it. When he returned to Mississippi he had $7,200 in his bank account.

He was on the Mississippi State University campus to enroll in classes. His mentor, Bill May, had gone there, and so had Ed's brother. As he walked across the campus on his first day, he struck up a conversation with a football player, who asked him what he planned to choose for a major.

When Ed replied "journalism," the athlete snorted: "We ain't got none of that down here. You need to go to Ole Miss." Ed called his mother, who contacted their state representative, George Payne Cossar, and soon after Ed was on a bus headed for Oxford.

The endorsement of Rep. Cossar must have carried some weight, for when the bus pulled into the station at Oxford, young Meek was met by two ranking officials from Ole Miss. One was Dr. Jim Webb, then Personnel Director, and the other was Dr. Samuel Talbert, chairman of the Department of Journalism. Dr. Sam took an immediate liking to Ed, offered him a $5-a-week part-time job in the department and, perhaps of more long-term significance to someone who had become so passionately interested in photography, promised him free and unlimited access to the journalism darkroom. Ed was prepared to work his way through Ole Miss.

There was the small problem of his studies, however, and that small problem almost did him in. He failed four of six courses his first semester—salvaging a C in his journalism class and another in ROTC. The second semester wasn't much better, and Robert Ellis, the Registrar, threatened to kick him out of school unless he could produce a B average in his twelve hours of summer session work. He and Becky were married that June 24, spent their wedding night in an apartment in the Ole Miss Village. Ed took an exam at 8 o'clock the next morning. His academic performance improved dramatically.

"Becky is the reason I made those grades," he said. "No doubt about that. She has been my motivating and solid-thinking partner ever since."

Ed and Helen Rebecca Wolfe had started dating in the ninth grade and were married as soon as she finished high school. The wedding cost was minimal—it had to be, since neither had much money. They used magnolia leaves, mostly, to decorate the Paynes Church at Charleston. Ed's savings, from his freelance work, went to buy a '49 Plymouth. Until then, he had hitchhiked home on vacations from Ole Miss. The dilapidated car had a hole in the muffler as well as a hole in the floorboard, unbeknownst to Ed and Becky, and fumes from the exhaust poured out to such an extent that a police car pulled the newlyweds over. Relieved that neither Mr. nor Mrs. Meek had been asphyxiated, the officer allowed them continue their journey to Oxford, so Ed wouldn't miss a critically important summer school exam the next morning.

Ed and Becky Meek. (Photo by Mikki Harris)

Becky Meek shared her husband's resourcefulness, his capacity for sustained hard work and, especially, his business sense. As the couple's money ran low, Becky invested $900 in a cosmetology course and within 10 months the couple had leased a shop. Becky had four others working for her and Ed, by his own admission, did the "marketing." The shop made money, but when Ed finished his degree he persuaded Becky to give up the shop and pursue her own educational goals. In time, and after giving birth to two babies, she got her master's degree in Special Education. When her graduate studies were completed, she was hired as a specialist in a state mental health agency, newly opened in Oxford, and worked there for 34 years.

Ed, meanwhile, had continued to plug away toward his own degree. Journalism students at that time could follow either of two tracks: A Bachelor of Arts program, which required, among much else, study of a foreign language. The other option, the Bachelor of Science degree, was heavily laden with courses in the School of Business. Fearful that he might never pass a foreign language course, Ed opted for the BSJ and, to his pleasant surprise, found he liked the business courses, the content of which he would later use to excellent advantage. Too, his favorite classes in journalism happened to be Dr. Sam's specialties, advertising and media management but Jere Hoar's classes in Feature Writing, Public Opinion and Law were the foundation that served him so well throughout his career. Dr. Sam gave him the human side of life and relationships, as Ed drove him here and there and as they visited early in the mornings, but Dr. Hoar discovered—and forced from him—abilities he never knew existed.

And though he would one day become a public relations man, Meek considered himself first and foremost a journalist. "I always felt that way. I never lied to a newspaperman," he said, carefully adding "but I may not have volunteered everything either."

One of Dr. Talbert's goals was to establish a chapter of journalism's professional society, Sigma Delta Chi. (The organization, open to students as well as practicing journalists, later became the Society of Professional Journalists.) Meek was a founding member of the Ole Miss chapter and served for two years as its president. Later he was the primary organizer of the Mississippi professional chapter, which at one time boasted 320 members and was known as one of the most active in that national society.

He supported himself through Ole Miss largely by writing and selling articles and photographs as a freelancer. He and another energetic classmate, Larry Speakes of Merigold, Mississippi, established themselves as "stringers" for newspapers interested in news from Ole Miss and Oxford. (A "stringer" is a freelance writer who submits articles to various publications and is normally paid by the column-inch length of each piece. Typically, each month the writer would paste together all the articles he or she had produced for each paper during that time and mail the paper his "string." The length of each string determined that month's pay.) Speakes and Meek, as they called themselves, generated so much Ole Miss news that the administration actually provided them office space in the Lyceum.

Long before recycling became fashionable, Speakes and Meek had developed it into an art form. Meek would send an article to, say, the Jackson *Daily News*. Then rewrite it, and, if necessary, provide a different picture, and send it to another paper—and get paid twice. Speakes was a stringer for the Memphis *Commercial Appeal* and a number of other papers. Meek wrote for the Mississippi Press Association, which circulated articles to member papers. Then, to camouflage the fact that Speakes and Meek were, in effect, a writing factory, the two overachieving undergraduates began to write under different names. For the Jackson *Daily News*, he used the by-line "Jim Roberts." For United Press International he used Edwin Meek. When he added the Birmingham *News* to his client list, he used his nickname from

151

high school, Budgie Meek. Once the *News* editor called and asked "Who the hell is Budgie Meek?" Meek explained that this was the nickname given him as a boy by his older brother. The editor told him Budgie was not a real name but he would come up with something else and hung up the phone. The next day there was a page one story under the by-line of Ed Meek. That name stuck, though his later bosses, chancellors J. D. Williams and Porter Fortune, never called him anything but Budgie. Meek's whirlwind energy and drive carried over to his studies. In one summer term, he took an independent study course in feature writing from Dr. Talbert. The first day, Meek asked Talbert what would be expected of him. Dr. Sam replied that, since there were about 30 days of that summer session, Ed's assignment was to write and sell an article a day, 30 in all. Incredibly, with the team of Speakes and Meek operating at top speed, Ed got it done. Later, Dr. Sam told him somewhat apologetically that when he assigned that article-a-day schedule he was only joking. But if Meek had mastered the craft of producing in quantity, he was also learning something about quality. "Jere Hoar forced me to learn to study and to write," Meek said. "He busted my buns but I made A's in Feature Writing, Public Opinion, and Law, as I recall, and for me that was one hell of an achievement." Understandably proud of that, he was also proud of some other honors he won as a student, especially when he was named "Graduate of the Year" by the journalism society, Sigma Delta Chi.

Meek was awarded his bachelor's degree in 1961. The campus was in turmoil at that time in the wake of the admission of James Meredith, the first African American to be enrolled at the University of Mississippi. Meredith's application, like the previous applications from other African Americans, had been unalterably opposed by the state's political power structure, and, as a result, necessarily rejected by the university. Unlike previous black applicants, however, Meredith stubbornly refused to back down. And he had the law on his side. He was qualified and would be admitted. His appearance in Oxford triggered angry protests and even riots. Federal troops were mobilized to insure Meredith's safety, and the United States Department of Justice, and even the White House, became deeply embroiled in the confrontation involving this one courageous and determined young African American man.

When Meredith arrived on campus, Meek was a student worker in the university's public relations office. He and Larry Speakes covered the rallies and the riots, which got bloody and resulted in the death of one journalist, one of many foreign correspondents on the scene. Meredith and Ole Miss were big news around the world. A teletype was provided for Speakes and Meek in the Lyceum. Too, the Associated Press provided the first AP photo transmitter ever installed on a college campus. The two men knew—or soon learned—how to cover a big story, and to cover it well.

Meek took perhaps the most famous photograph of the Meredith saga. It was of James Meredith, neatly dressed in a brown suit and tie, sitting alone in a classroom his first day as a student. Others in the class had walked out in protest, but Meredith quietly sat at his student desk. The photo perfectly captures the solemnity, the dignity and the loneliness of that poignant scene.[188] Journalists had been barred from entering the building, but Meek, his camera concealed under a trench coat, told the guards, truthfully, that he was a student and they let him in.

Ed remained at Ole Miss to work on his master's degree. In 1963 on the day it was to be awarded James Meredith was also being graduated. In order to report on the event Meek reluctantly chose not to walk in the procession, where he would have likely been positioned very near to Meredith and could not see or photograph him.

After his graduation, Meek was offered a job as a science writer in the Ole Miss public relations office. His salary would be $7,200 a year—less, actually, than he and Larry Speakes were hauling in from their freelance work. Soon after he went full-time with university, he became, at 24, director of the university's public relations office, and charged with the uphill task of helping restore the Ole Miss reputation, which was in tatters after the ugly confrontation over James Meredith and integration. Meek was thus the youngest ever to hold that directorship. The chancellor, Dr. J. D. Williams, put it to Ed this way: "I am the only person in the administration who thinks you can do this job, and it is yours. Don't let me down."

He didn't. Meek's hard work and personal contacts generated reams of favorable publicity for the university. Aggressively, he visited media offices throughout the region. At one point, he recalls, "I knew just about every member of the press community in Mississippi, and much of Tennessee, Arkansas, Louisiana and Alabama—largely because Dr. Sam (Talbert) dragged me to meetings everywhere."

After a decade as director of PR at Ole Miss, Meek decided he was likely to spend the rest of his career in higher education, and that meant he ought to get his doctoral degree. He took evening classes at Ole Miss but was not admitted to the doctoral program because his score on the Graduate Record Examination was 10 points below the minimum required for acceptance. He took the test again, with the same result. His new boss, Chancellor Porter Fortune, had come to Ole Miss from Mississippi Southern (now the University of Southern Mississippi). Dr. Fortune telephoned the president there, Dr. William David McCain, with a recommendation that got Meek admitted to that doctoral program.

In a bumpy Volkswagen that was without air conditioning, Meek made the 300-miles-plus drive from Oxford to Hattiesburg. Dr. McCain, a former general, met him. Then, and in a surplus Army Jeep, the President conducted him on a personal tour of the campus and authorized him to stay in the top floor of the institution's new football dormitory. The floor was unoccupied except for one other student, Jim Singleton, an African American from New

Orleans. The two became good friends, largely because each wanted to know more about the other's race. At the end of the summer, when the dorm was closed to them, Meek and Singleton rented a one-bedroom apartment and slept in the same bed. This, Meek said, proved to be a life-changing experience for him. So was his class work under Dr. Gerald Flannery, a demanding professor whose assignments kept Meek in the library from the time it opened, at 7 a.m., until class began at 6 that evening. "He was a visionary," Meek said of Dr. Flannery. "He cultivated my interest in the future and technology and its implications in our society."

Meek was able to use his higher education credits from Ole Miss as a minor. He wrote his dissertation on a famous case of that time, *United Church of Christ v. Federal Communications Commission*[189] in which a powerful television station in Jackson, WLBT, had its license revoked by federal authorities because some of the content in the station's news and public affairs programming was held to have racist overtones. A new, hastily assembled group of local business leaders (and mostly amateurs to television station management) was awarded the license. Meek was named to the station's reorganized operating board. The new station managers, some of whom had little to no experience as broadcasters, revamped the programming, brought in new people—many of them African Americans—and gave the Mississippi capital city a different type of television station. And still made a profit. One innovation was to add a daily program for children, and that served, among much else, to bring Meek into contact with the Children's Television Workshop, producer of "Sesame Street." He was the Workshop's Mississippi representative when Big Bird was developed.

Meek's doctorate, conferred in 1976, was Southern Mississippi's first in the field of mass communication. As he exited the stage, he opened the rolled up diploma sheet and found a note: "Atta Boy!" He looked back at President McCain, who winked at him.

After his year in residence at Hattiesburg, Meek was able to complete his course work by commuting from Oxford. During those long, hot rides in his VW, Meek kept a legal pad at his side and jotted down business ideas that raced through his brain. One was for a mini-storage operation, which, when he opened it, was the first for Oxford.

Another idea he had was how maybe to work around those grueling drives between Oxford, in the top part of the state, and Hattiesburg, in the bottom. At the time, Southern Airways operated a small commuter service linking Oxford and Greenwood and Meridian and Hattiesburg. Meek wrote Graden Hall, vice president of the airline, advising him that Southern Airways needed a part-time public relations man in Mississippi, and he, Meek, was ideally suited for that job. Hall responded by sending Meek an employment contract. Southern would pay him $25 a month ("He must have been talking to Bill May," Meek observed.) But the deal also provided him a pass that permitted

154

Meek and his family to fly free, and with seat priority, anywhere. He kept that pass for 10 years, even after Southern Airways was bought by Republic and later Northwest Airlines. The world-wide travels were nice, but to Meek the sweetest flights of all were those between Oxford and Hattiesburg.

Meek's next business venture was a furniture mart in Tupelo, a thriving town some 40 miles away, a place where several woodworking and furniture operations were situated. Meek operated the trade mart out of Oxford for a couple of years. The Market did work from day one, Meek made $360,000 net profit from the first market and there were two a year. However, locals with more money took it away from him. He came home, developed more magazines, and the trade show experience in Tupelo caused him to develop show properties throughout the nation, the largest in Las Vegas. Ideally, the market would have been situated nearer Memphis, a far larger market, more easily accessible, and with plenty of hotels. But Dr. Sam had introduced Meek to George McClain when he was 18-19, and McClain's devotion to the Tupelo community, and his creation of CREATE motivated Meek to build the market in Tupelo, rather than Southaven. The Tupelo Furniture Mart—in a 2.5 million square foot facility—attracted manufacturers, wholesalers and retailers from far and wide and helped make Ed Meek a wealthy man.

In the meantime, Meek was developing a number of side businesses—an advertising agency, warehouses, an educational publishing group. His restless, curious nature revealed communication gaps among various career fields, so he launched a series of "niche magazines," as they are called, targeted to highly specific audiences. His first was the *Mississippi Pharmacist*. Ed and Becky and their kids cut and pasted up the pages, laying them out on their kitchen table. *Satellite TV Opportunities*, the second publication, did well, sometimes averaging 260 pages per issue. When the earlier version of home satellites failed (the government's new regulations closed a loophole that radically changed the industry), Meek acquired *Nightclub & Bar*, a struggling magazine that had been founded by one of his former students. The business grew swiftly, and Meek's publishing operation launched or revitalized other niche magazines, including *Oxford Magazine*, a local tourist publication; *Mississippi Pharmacist*, for the state pharmacy association; *KuBand World* (for satellite users as the market moved from C-Band to the more efficient and greater capacity Ku-Band dish); *Beverage Retailer*, for wine and liquor store owners; *Bar Product News*; *Satellite Product News; Service Tips* and *Restaurant Marketing* and *Salud*, an English/Spanish language hospitality magazine. At one time or another, there were 11 magazines produced by his company.

All this while he was director of public information for Ole Miss.

These commercial successes met with the strong disapproval of his immediate superior in the Lyceum, who summoned Meek to his office in the Lyceum and told him in no uncertain terms that he was expected to devote himself to the university seven days a week, 24 hours a day. Meek responded innocently by asking: Those large herds of cattle his boss, and at least one Ole Miss vice president, owned: were they raising and selling cattle as a hobby? Or were they business operations? He never got any more flak after that.

Dr. Porter Fortune, the chancellor and Meek's ultimate boss, seconded him out for a year to work in Jackson for Gov. Cliff Finch. Then Dr. Fortune nominated him for an American Council on Education fellowship. Thirty ACE fellowships, highly coveted, are awarded each year to outstanding young academics who seem destined to become executives at colleges and universities. Each fellow devotes that year to working with, and observing, top-level administrators at another campus. Meek spent his fellowship year at the University of Tennessee.

After Meek got his doctorate, the Academic Vice President, Dr. Charles Noyes, suggested he might do some teaching. Delighted, Meek taught a class in public relations, offered by the Department of Journalism, for several semesters, and was able to convey his own work ethic and enthusiasm to his students.

"Ed Meek was and is a visionary in communications," recalls Kevin Seddon ('88), who later started his own advertising/public relations business. "He introduced entire industries to the Internet early. . . He taught me how all media and promotional disciplines interrelate and must all be considered in business communications."[190]

"When I stepped into Dr. Meek's PR class, my love of Ole Miss went into a new stratosphere," said Bill Glenn ('92). Meek assigned him his first press release. It got published, and Glenn went on from there. "I will forever be grateful to Ed Meek for giving me the opportunity."[191]

Harriet Riley ('81) recalls a high point in her undergraduate days: "I was lucky enough to have an internship in public relations under Ed Meek."[192]

"Dr. Meek was indeed a role model for me and he pushed all the students he met to pursue a career that they enjoy rather than what is acceptable to others," remembers Emily Gilleylen-McMillan ('82), who became a broadcast sales and publicity person.[193]

Gigi McMurray ('88), who went into church communications work, boasts of keeping "an old worn-out t-shirt with the beautiful logo "Ole Miss . . . Dr. Meek gave me this shirt after he helped me get my first job. He also had a part in my second and third jobs. Dr. Ed Meek taught me one course during my time at Ole Miss but he impacts me today. He taught me by modeling hospitality and networking and kindness."[194]

Before he met his first class, Meek hastily dashed to the campus bookstore to buy a public relations text. He had never read one before. But he knew his business and he knew how to relate to young people.

His classes were relaxed and informal. At his insistence, students called him "Ed." And, as Sam and Fran Talbert had done, he and Becky frequently hosted student parties in their home.

"One of my great pleasures, and perhaps my greatest contribution as an academic, was my commitment to help students get through school, as others did for me," Meek said. "And to help them find their places in society." He helped literally hundreds of students and former students get jobs, writing letters and making phone calls and providing personal evaluations, a practice he continued long after his teaching days ended.

A chronicle of Ed Meek's good works goes on and on. Examples:

- He did much to promote to a national audience the artistry of Theora Hamblett. Born in Paris, Mississippi, in 1893, she taught school for 20 years before moving to Oxford in the late 1930s. She ran a boardinghouse for Ole Miss students and worked as a seamstress until she was 57 years old. Then she began a serious career as a painter. Though she had taken a few art courses at the university, she was essentially self-taught, developing her own pointillist technique, using dots of vivid color instead of brush strokes to create her scenes. Her paintings--of scenes from her childhood, the Mississippi countryside, religious visions, everyday life in the South-were unique as well as brilliant. Ed Meek worked with Miss Hamblett to publish four books of her paintings, books which helped gain for her a national reputation. He also persuaded her to leave her estate, including valuable paintings, to the University of Mississippi after her death in 1977.

- An Eagle scout himself, Meek has worked with Oxford scout troops throughout his adult life and for more than 20 years he served on the board of directors for the Yocona Area Boy Scout Council.

- He was instrumental in getting legislation passed to create the Small Business Development Center, an agency which now has its counterpart in every state. Meek envisioned this as a counterweight to the Department of Agriculture, which receives billions in federal aid each year, though it represents only about three percent of the population. His lobbying effort took him to Washington, where he worked with Congressman Jamie Whitten, and persuaded Ole Miss Chancellor Porter Fortune to testify in behalf of the bill. This small business agency and its offshoots would support literally thousands of enterprises across the country.

- While in Washington, he spent time with Mississippi Senator James Eastland, soon persuading him to push to bring the small business bill, then stuck in committee, to the Senate floor. Meek actually wrote the request and got Senator Eastland to sign it. After that, the Senator said "It's after five, let's have a drink." He pulled a bottle of Jack Daniel's out of his desk drawer. "We had a snort or two," Meek said, "and that bill passed the next day. I swear he had no idea of what that bill was."

- Meek's ability to work with legislators and the media had not gone unnoticed by key figures in Mississippi's power structure. One major player, Tom Hederman, publisher of the influential *Clarion Ledger* as well as *The Daily News* in Jackson, selected Meek to become press secretary to Senator Eastland, a political ally. Meek declined, but suggested instead that the job go to his close friend from undergraduate days, Larry Speakes. After his years at Ole Miss, Speakes had been editor and general manager of three Mississippi newspapers. Articulate and smart, he moved comfortably into the Washington scene, and a few years later was named White House Press Secretary for President Ronald Reagan. He served in that high-profile, demanding position from 1981 to 1987.

For his part, Meek went back home and stayed there. In 1998, he retired from Ole Miss. He had racked up 38 years of service, two of which were unused sick leave. Soon after, he was presented with the Governor's Distinguished Mississippian Award. It could serve as a fitting climax to an amazing career. But, for Ed Meek, his most spectacular, and most prosperous, years were still ahead.

Meek's business enterprises, which included an advertising agency as well as a slew of niche magazines, were making money. A good bit of it, but not as much as Ed and Becky thought. "I have to confess that I am not good at keeping up with money, nor do I enjoy doing it," Meek admitted. So he hired a friend, a former banker, to handle the books. One night he got an anonymous phone call, suggesting that he investigate his bookkeeper. He did, and found the man had siphoned off profits, not only from the Meeks but from other businesses in the area. The bookkeeper went to jail, and Becky took charge of the accounting. The lesson was learned, but it cost the Meeks an estimated half a million dollars to learn it.

Once the bookkeeping got to be honest and accurate, Meek discovered he was now well off financially. He also discovered, through his niche magazines and the audiences they reached, the substantial fortune that could be made by producing trade shows. His first trade show dealt with the home satellite industry. After that, he applied what he had learned about bars and restaurants to put on a huge trade show in Las Vegas. That led to highly successful trade shows in Atlantic City, Chicago, Nashville, Orlando, Atlanta and New Orleans. One of his Las Vegas trade shows drew some 34,000 attendees and was said to be the largest food and beverage trade show in the Western World. The Meek business had become a hot property.

Though older and wiser and richer, Ed Meek had not materially changed. He was a little grayer, a little heavier, but still the unpretentious, cheerful, smiling, boyish personage that literally thousands of Mississippians had come to know and like. As late as 2011 he was still driving a car that was 9 years old. Or a pickup truck that was 18.

In most respects, he was like everybody else. But a couple of things set him apart: He worked hard, harder than most, and he always seemed to be a step or two ahead of the curve.

Acutely aware, as always of economic and media trends, and prodded by a gentle reminder from Becky that they were no longer in the blush of youth, Meek decided it might be time to cash out.

He and Becky spent three years, then, getting their affairs in order and interviewing companies that wanted to buy the business. Ultimately they sold to the Questex Media Group in Newton, Massachusetts, for millions of dollars. The Meeks stipulated that the headquarters would remain in Oxford, and that Ed would remain in control of the operations. The last year under Meek the company netted $4.73 million, the 23rd straight year of profitability. Then the new owners told him, "you're a good ole boy, Ed, but you can't take it to the next level and we want you to step aside." He did. And that "next level" turned out to be downward. Precipitously downward. The next year profits shrank to $770,000 and the year after that the new owners filed for bankruptcy. Meek took no satisfaction from seeing his know-it-all buyers fail, and besides, their bankruptcy cost him millions in management and consultant fees, broken promises that courts would have to adjudicate.

Still, the Meeks had come long way since that wedding day journey to Oxford more than 40 years earlier, when they miraculously survived the noxious fumes from an ancient Plymouth with a perforated muffler and a hole in the floorboard. They had worked hard. They had created a family and a fortune. They established trust funds for their children and allocated generous amounts to their church (Oxford-University United Methodist) and to the Yocona Area Council of the Boy Scouts of America. And they had given the Ed and Becky Meek School of Journalism and New Media the largest endowment of any school at the University of Mississippi, an endowment that placed it in the top tier of journalism schools throughout the nation. The entire estate, including a substantial art collection will go to the school.[195]

As a young student he had helped build the tradition of Ole Miss Journalism, and as a faculty member he had enhanced it. Then, as the school's benefactor, he had provided the wherewithal to make sure the professional and academic community could see just how good that program was, and could be.

The Meek School Era Begins

Old Light, New Light

Dean Will Norton

When Dean Will Norton returned to Ole Miss in 2009, it was to a campus that had been transformed, as if by magic, largely through the inspired leadership of Chancellor Robert C. Khayat.

If ever a man was born to do a specific job, Robert Khayat must have been destined to lead the University of Mississippi. Most of his life had been spent with some connection to Ole Miss. And while many universities are loath to promote from within—the fear some have of inbreeding and the absence of new ideas—Robert Khayat's knowledge of the institution and of Mississippi gave him insight and confidence that fitted him perfectly for the chancellorship. His credentials were impeccable and his leadership proved to be sure-handed and masterful.

As an undergraduate at Ole Miss, he had been a football star, a lineman on the powerful football teams of Coach John Vaught, an all-conference catcher on the best baseball team in the university's history. The Washington Redskins signed him after graduation, and he played several seasons of professional football. Then came law school at Ole Miss, followed by a Master of Laws degree from Yale. Hired to join the Law faculty at Ole Miss, he was soon chosen the school's outstanding professor. And as the years passed, he taught, and influenced, many of the young men and women, lawyers-to-be, who would develop into key movers and shakers in the state's power structure. Eventually, Dr. Khayat would be promoted to the central administration, and in 1995 he was named chancellor.

161

Then big things happened. Among them:

- Research and development grants shot up, topping $100 million eight years in a row.
- Enrollment increased by nearly 44 percent and minority enrollment by more than 78 percent.
- Phi Beta Kappa, the nation's leading liberal arts scholarship society, awarded Ole Miss a chapter. After years of rejecting Ole Miss, the elite society finally acknowledged the academic soundness of the institution and welcomed Ole Miss into the ranks of the nation's premier universities.
- The endowment grew from $114.3 million to $472.4 million, an increase of more than 300 percent.
- The university's operating budget grew from less than $500 million to nearly $1.5 billion, and the payroll nearly tripled.
- New facilities on the Oxford campus included a $50 million law center (the university would later name it for Robert Khayat); a $46 million residential college; a $30 million natural products research center; a $19.6 research park; an $18.5 million baseball stadium expansion; a $16 million Center for Manufacturing Excellence, a $12 million basketball practice center. He enjoyed comparably spectacular success in strengthening the university's Medical School at Jackson.[196]

He was, in short, a superb fundraiser, and he proved to be a particular friend of the Department of Journalism.

Aware that Charles Overby, CEO of the Freedom Forum, maintained strong ties to Ole Miss, Khayat journeyed to Florida to call on Al Neuharth, whose genius had built the Gannett Co. into the country's largest newspaper group. Long since retired, Neuharth still wielded enormous power with the Freedom Forum, a foundation built with Gannett profits.

Chancellor Robert Khayat, University of Mississippi 1995-2009

Khayat was in the midst of making a pitch for something to honor Charles Overby when Neuharth broke in: "What took you so long?"[197]

Thus was born what would become the Overby Center for Southern Journalism and Politics, a $5 million addition to the journalism building.

Modest and unassuming, Charles Overby at first resisted having the facility named for him. But Neuharth and Khayat held their ground.

Then, on a visit to the campus while the Center was under construction, Overby did journalism yet another favor: "This new building will make the journalism building (Farley Hall, which now had some age on it) look bad," Overby said, in effect.

"I've seen this sort of thing happen before." Khayat agreed.

"Then I'll go to the Legislature and get a half million to renovate Farley Hall," he said.[198] And he delivered.

Dedicated in 2008, the Overby Center provided 16,000 square feet of conference space, a fully equipped, state-of-the-art, 215-seat auditorium, and multipurpose areas for meetings and research. Its News Wall, linked to the Freedom Forum's fabulous Newseum in Washington, featured nine large-screen TV monitors continuously showing current cable news programs and the front pages of a dozen or more Southern daily newspapers. Together, the new Overby Center for Southern Journalism and Politics and the beautifully renovated Farley Hall gave Ole Miss quarters and facilities that would be the envy of journalism programs everywhere.

But journalism was still a department. To some in the academy, titles don't mean much. "I don't care if they call us a Closet of Journalism," declared one university department chairman, "so long as they give us the support we need." That, however, is distinctly a minority viewpoint. For most, the difference between a department and a school is the difference between, say, in gridiron terms, a first down and a touchdown. First downs are good, but only touchdowns put points on the scoreboard. In the academy, a "department" is typically lumped in with many other departments, all having secondary status, all competing equally—or unequally—under associate deans and a dean. A separate "school," however, has its own dean and, more important, a seat at the head table, the table where priorities and budgets are decided.

2010: The Delta Project included a combination of photographers, reporters and videographers. The publication they produced, *The Roads of Broken Dreams*, won a Kennedy Award.

Almost since the day of its creation in 1946, the men who headed journalism at Ole Miss dreamed their department would one day become a school. More than half a century later, the dream came true. Ed Meek's wealth and love for Ole Miss, and Chancellor Robert Khayat's support and influence, made it happen.

The situation developed this way: Ed Meek needed to hire more graphic design people for his hugely prosperous printing business. The qualified persons he sought simply were not available, at least not available nearby, and the young people he had interviewed seemed not to have yet realized the enormous potential of FaceBook, YouTube and other social media. Figuring other publishers were facing the same problem, Meek shared his concern with his old friend, Robert Khayat. The chancellor immediately understood and agreed. Meek offered to give Ole Miss a million dollars to hire teachers of the new technologies. "Make it six million," Khayat replied, "and you can have a school." Meek agreed to an initial gift of $5.3 million, and Khayat agreed to support the creation of a school.

The official name, given at the announcement ceremony in May 2007, was the Ed and Becky Meek School of Journalism and New Media. Sweetening the deal, Ed and Becky Meek rewrote their wills to endow the school with many millions more.

"Becky and I feel we owe the university so much," Meek said. "We are delighted to be able to repay Ole Miss a very small part of the very large debt our family owes for the great opportunities the university has given to three generations."[199]

Meek leavened his gratitude for the past with a clear-eyed view toward the future.

"The (journalism) profession as a whole was caught with its pants down," Meek said of dramatic technological change in the ways communication was transmitted. "The 'New Media' part of the name means learning to use all of the opportunities offered by the Internet, which, in our country, is still in its infancy. . .The backbone of public and private communication has totally changed. Our students need to know how to use it."[200]

Job One now was to find a dean. Dr. Samir Husni, who had ably served several stretches as department chair on an interim basis,[201] had earned a global reputation as a most respected authority in his particular field, was thought to be too uniquely valuable as "Mr. Magazine" to remove him from full-time teaching. A national search ensued for a professional administrator, one comfortable within the academic hierarchy, and possessing the skill and energy and innovative ideas necessary to take Ole Miss into the top tier of journalism schools nationally. When, after several entreaties, Will Norton finally expressed interest, the central administrators at Ole Miss knew they had found their man.

By this time, 2009, Norton had been dean at Nebraska for nearly two decades. During those years he had successfully pushed for a new, state-of-the-art building and had overseen the design and construction of it. The College of Journalism and Mass Communications he headed at Nebraska was nationally respected—being selected one of 12 Carnegie-Knight schools. Norton had been elected to the presidency of the two leading professional associations and was acknowledged as to be one of the top journalism administrators in the nation.

He had also reached retirement age and was ready to step aside at Nebraska. His wife Susan, who had been raised in Oxford, had endured bone-chilling winters at Lincoln and was anxious to return home. Their son and daughter, William and Elaine, were educated and out of the nest, pursuing careers of their own. The school of journalism that Norton had hoped for at Ole Miss had finally come into being. So when he was offered the deanship, he elected to accept it. To his friends and fellow deans around the country, the move from Ole Miss to Nebraska and back again was known as "Will's remarkable U-turn."

There was but one regret: "I'm just sad that I'm not younger," he said, soon after taking over at the Meek School. "The possibilities here are enormous. I'd love to be alive 25 years from now to see what this place is going to be."[202]

Norton's energy level, already high, seemed to kick into yet another passing gear when he arrived back on the Oxford campus. "I had 19 years at Nebraska," he confided to a friend, "I don't have 20 years here."[203]

So he hit the ground running. Within months of his arrival back in Oxford, Norton had seen the Meek School:

- Successfully undergo a reaccreditation examination and visit.

165

- Launch a depth reporting team to study people and conditions in the Mississippi Delta. The project, entitled *The Roads of Broken Dreams*, resulted in publications and a documentary and won the Robert F. Kennedy award in 2010 as the outstanding collegiate journalism achievement in the nation.
- Place, for the first time in years, in the Hearst College Journalism Awards national contests in which students from accredited journalism schools compete.
- Developed, and secured approval for, an Integrated Marketing Communication degree, giving students at the Meek School an additional, and promising, career option.
- Took home multiple awards in both the Society of Professional Journalists Mark of Excellence and the Southeastern Conference Journalism competitions.[204]

2010: The Newswatch crew included: Ashley Phillips, station manager; Tricia Forbes, news director; Stuart Johnson, assignment editor; Sally Nicely and Brittany Hemphill, producers; and Jacob Newton, sports director.

Perhaps most important of all, Norton was able to add more outstanding professionals to a tenured faculty of accomplished media professionals of significant academic achievement:

Assistant Dean Charlie Mitchell, who had taught journalism at Ole Miss in the 1980s, was executive editor of the *Vicksburg Post,* and a past president of the Mississippi Press Association. Though he held a law degree and was active in the Bar Association, he was more at home in journalism, where he won awards for his reporting from Iraq and on Hurricane Katrina, a storm which had devastated New Orleans and much of southern Mississippi. Even after rejoining the faculty in 2010, he continued to write his weekly column, "Conversations," which was carried by more than 20 newspapers in the region. Few newspaper people in the region were better known, or better liked.

Patricia Thompson, who took over as director of student media, brought dazzling credentials for the job with her. She had been a staff writer for *The Washington Post*, among other dailies, and was an editor at *The San Jose Mercury News,* and part of the team that won that paper's Pulitzer in 1990. She also had taught at Northwestern University's Medill School of Journalism, one of the nation's finest.

Bill Rose, an Ole Miss graduate whose career in journalism spanned 40 years. Much of it was spent at the *Miami Herald*, where he was an award-winning reporter and editor. When he retired from day-to-day journalism, he was managing editor of the *Palm Beach Post*. Back at Ole Miss, he co-led, with Pat Thompson, the award-winning Delta Project.

2013: Kayla Vise with Bill Rose after an interview with Southern Fried Comics owner in Hattiesburg, Miss

Mitchell, Thompson and Rose joined a faculty that already included such respected veteran professionals as:

Curtis Wilkie, an Ole Miss alum ('63) who first worked at *The Clarksdale Press Register*, then went to *The Boston Globe*. A first-rate reporter who established the *Globe's* Middle East Bureau in Jerusalem in the 1980s, he covered the Israeli invasion of Lebanon, as well as the first Gulf War, among many other hostile actions in that troubled part of the world. Later he covered politics, including several Presidential campaigns, for the *Globe* and served as chief of the paper's Washington bureau. He has written any number of articles for national magazines, and two significant books: *Dixie: A Personal Odyssey Through Events that Shaped the Modern South*[205] and *The Fall of the House of Zeus*.[206] The latter is the story of the flamboyant Mississippi lawyer, Dickie Scruggs, who made millions by winning judgments against the tobacco industry and other corporate defendants—he was known nationally as "the king of torts"—before later being convicted and jailed for jury tampering. Wilkie's even-handed, thorough analysis of the Dickie Scruggs career was well received by critics, and the author/professor was sought out for interviews by national television networks as well as newspapers and magazines

In 2002, Wilkie returned to Ole Miss and soon after was appointed to the Kelly G. Cook chair in the Department of Journalism. Later he was named the first Overby Fellow with the Overby Center as the department became the Meek School of Journalism and New Media.

While some outstanding professionals may regard teaching as simply an opportunity to tell, and re-tell, personal war stories, Curtis Wilkie worked hard at teaching, and proved to be good at it.

"I would turn in a story or op-ed to Curtis," recalls Emmett H. McClary ('07), "and no matter what he thought of my opinion or style he would always say 'this is good but it is not as good as it could be if you would do this and this and more of this.' Curtis would never say 'that's awful wrong or stupid (although lots of our writing was all of those things). That made more of an impression on me than any instructor I've ever had."[207]

Mary Margaret Miller ('07) writes that "Curtis Wilkie helped me to think critically about the world around me and showed me that writing can not only inform a community, but can change lives."[208]

Though he had become a celebrity, the bearded, cheerful Wilkie never lost the down-home folksiness of the Mississippi Delta, where he had been born. He had honed his own journalistic skills at Ole Miss, and now was giving new generations of students the opportunity to do the same thing.

Joe Atkins, who had been Congressional correspondent for Gannett News Service as well as a reporter and columnist for many years before joining the Ole Miss faculty in 1990. "Ace" Atkins continued to write a statewide column, was the author of a book on labor issues in the South and a contributor to a book on media ethics. His articles, especially on ethics and labor matters, have appeared in some of the country's leading publications.

Jeanni Atkins (no relation), who directed the graduate program for 15 years, is a leading authority on matters dealing with freedom of information. Her research has resulted in papers she presented at many national and international conferences. She helped found the Mississippi Center for Freedom of Information.

Debora Halpern Wenger, who was a broadcast news professional for 17 years, conducts research in the area of convergence media presentation, and leads multimedia training sessions in newsrooms around the country.[209]

And more than a dozen other skilled professionals, including several highly promising, and highly recruited, young members of the Meek School faculty joined a strong faculty. Chancellor Dan Jones' support was essential to early successes.

2011: Norton and Overby in conversation at Overby's retirement dinner on the grounds at Rowan Oak. Photo by Robert Jordan

May 14, 2011, was graduation day at Ole Miss. That Saturday morning, there was a campus-wide commencement ceremony, and for it several thousand visitors gathered under cloudless skies, in the Grove. In the afternoon, the colleges and schools held smaller, and much more personal, ceremonies honoring those whose studies had been completed under their auspices. It was the first-ever such separate ceremony for graduates of the Meek School. The setting was the Ford Theater auditorium, a beautiful facility, and it was filled for the occasion. The commencement speaker was Dan Rather, former anchor of the CBS Evening News and a giant in broadcast journalism. As each degree was conferred, the recipient walked across the stage into a receiving line composed of the professors who had mentored their progress that led up to that moment—and a handshake and word of encouragement from Dan Rather.

The new graduates already had jobs, most of them, or plans for graduate work or, in some cases, foreign travel. They were proud of their diplomas and, despite the uncertainty in the media industries, clearly confident about the future and their role in it. No matter what may be the platform or medium of presentation, some of them said, in effect, there will always be a demand for content. And we can and will provide it.

The ceremony, and the infusion of new talent it signified, was impressive. By any standard of measurement, the Meek School's first two years had been a rousing success.

More to the point, the groundwork had been well laid for more success in the years ahead. The Meek School faculty had adopted a Strategic Plan, listing immediate goals of improving student writing, developing more diversity in the student body and faculty, and long-range goals, such as expanding interdisciplinary partnerships and enhancing student perspective on international issues.

2013 Kennedy award winners for Belize publication (left to right): Aubrey Killion, Cain Madden, Katie Williamson, Margaret Ann Morgan and Patricia Thompson.

The Plan also proclaimed the school's core values, and foremost among these was ardent support of Freedom of Expression:

We foster freedom of expression by helping students understand the relationship between free speech and a democracy, and that understanding is at the heart of the mission of the Meek School of Journalism and New Media.[210]

170

Other shared values included a reaffirmation of the importance of teaching excellence and a commitment to embrace the changes inevitably ahead for the communications industries in the ways information and ideas are presented to the increasingly fragmented public.

But, facilities and faculty notwithstanding, the underlying strength of the Meek School—as it had been for the old Department of Journalism at Ole Miss—would be the quality and inner drive of its students: Young men and women like Elizabeth Vowell ('11), who had learned how to tell a news story, and were undaunted by the effort required to do it well.

As part of the national award-winning Delta Project, she sensed "the only way to get a feel for that hard-luck region was from the air." She talked a crop-duster pilot into taking her up. "We wanted a shot of the whole area," she said, and she didn't quit until she got it.

The history of Ole Miss journalism is the story of many like Elizabeth Vowell of Quitman, Mississippi, who knew where they wanted to go and pushed themselves hard to get there. The Meek School of Journalism and New Media, like the Department of Journalism that preceded it, was merely an incubator. But it would be hard to find a better one.

As early as the 1970s a "light bulb" joke was making the rounds in Mississippi: Question: How many Mississippians does it take to change a light bulb? Answer: Ten. One person actually to change the bulb, and nine other folks to stand around and talk about how good the old light bulb was. The fact that Mississippians told that joke on themselves reflects a certain degree of self-assurance: We kid about the past, they were saying, but deep down we respect it too. The new light bulb, the Meek School, well staffed, well equipped, and well funded, would burn brighter, and would illuminate the lives and careers of many young men and women in the years ahead.

But that old light bulb, with far less candle power, had managed to do pretty well too.

Endnotes

Hotty Toddy

1. John Savage, then vice chancellor and comptroller, to the author, August 1973.
2. David G. Sansing, *The University of Mississippi: A Sesquicentennial History*, University Press of Mississippi (1999), 106.
3. Quoted by Libby Smith, *Arkansas Democrat-Gazette*, June 21, 2010.
4. Among them Willie Morris, Curtis Wilkie, Jere Hoar, and Joe Atkins, all of whom taught in the Ole Miss journalism program.
5. Dwight Garner, "Of Parties, Prose, and Football," *The New York Times*, October 16, 2011.
6. Charles W. Eagles, *The Price of Defiance: James Meredith and the Integration of Ole Miss*, University of North Carolina Press, (2009), 16.
7. Sansing, *op. cit.*, 183.
8. Janine Wilkes Dunlap, *The History of the Department of Journalism at the University of Mississippi*, 1947-1987, unpublished master's thesis, University of Mississippi, 1987, 14.
9. Elizabeth Shiver, interview with the author, May 11, 2010.
10. Eagles, *op. cit.*, 21. It would be wrong, however, to characterize all Ole Miss students as sons and daughters of the wealthy. To the contrary, many are small town youths from relatively poor families, young men and women who see the University of Mississippi as their springboard to a better life.

Gerald Forbes

11. Janine Wilkes Dunlap, *The History of the Department of Journalism at the University of Mississippi, 1947-87*, unpublished master's thesis, University of Mississippi, 1988, 13.
12. ibid.
13. Betty Brenkert, *The Oxford Eagle*, March 22, 1984.
14. Clark Kerr, then president of the University of California, once remarked that "there is nothing more permanent on a college campus than a temporary building."
15. Dunlap, *op. cit.*, 19.
16. Gerald Forbes, annual administrative report, 1948.
17. Brenkert, *op. cit.*
18. *ibid.*
19. Albin J. Krebs, quoted in Dunlap, *op. cit.*, 31.

20. Elizabeth Shiver, interview with the author, May 10, 2010.
21. Shiver, Silver Em award speech, April 20, 2003.
22. Note to the author, May 10, 2010.
23. Dunlap, *op. cit.*, 23.
24. James A. Autry, note to the author, June 11, 2010.
25. Will Norton asked Forbes the reason for his resignation when Forbes returned to campus to celebrate the founding of MSPA. Interview with Norton, April 3, 2012.
26. Talbert, letter to Jere Hoar, dated April 29, 1956.
27. Talbert, letter to Jere Hoar, dated May 10, 1956.
28. ibid. Moeller said he "did not think it unwise" for Hoar to accept the Mississippi offer.
29. Two letters from Forbes and other historical materials may eventually be located in the Meek School records in the attic of Farley Hall. In 1986 Dr. Hoar turned them over to the then chairman when he retired from full time teaching, and cleared his desk. It had previously been the desk used by Dr. Forbes.
30. Forbes, letter to Jesse Phillips. The letter is not dated.

Samuel S. Talbert

31. Ed Meek to the author, November 1, 2010. Much of the description of Talbert came from a former student and later colleague, Dr. Jere Hoar, in interviews during the spring and summer, 2010.
32. Talbert to Hoar, undated letter, *c.* 1956
33. Peterson to the author, May 10, 2010.
34. Note to the author, March 30, 2010.
35. Dunlap, *op. cit.*, 18.
36. Talbert, *Annual Report*, 1957-58.
37. Note to the author, February 20, 2010.
38. Email from Nancy Mason, February 16, 2014.
39. A list of Silver Em awardees can be found in the Appendix. In 2004, the honor was officially renamed the Samuel S. Talbert Silver Em Award.
40. Hoar to the author, August 18, 2010.
41. *Commercial Appeal*, May 23, 1954.
42. *The Oxford Eagle,* October 19, 2010.
43.*ibid,* April 26, 1972.
44. *ibid.*

Jere Hoar

45. Quoted by Robert Hall, Southern Scribe web site, May 1, 2010. Much of the background information that follows stems from this source.

46. Of the $30 a month men earned, $25 was sent to their families.
47. "The Fugitives" refers to a Southern literary movement begun at Vanderbilt University.
48. Talbert, letter to Hoar, May 8, 1956.
49. Talbert, letter to Hoar, April 29, 1956.
50. Talbert letter to Hoar, May 10.
51. Knowing Prof. Moeller well, Hoar considered the recommendation lukewarm.
52. At coffee on one occasion, Talbert was addressing his colleagues at length, and with specificity, on what goes on in private areas of New Orleans gay bars. At one point he called for confirmation from his sidekick, Gale Denley. "Ain't that right, Denley?" he demanded. Denley threw up his hands. "I've got no idea!" he said.
53. Another summer would be spent at Iowa. The Ph.D. would not be awarded until 1960.
54. *The Journal of Psychology, Sociology and Social Research, Journalism Quarterly,* and *The Journal of Educational Sociology.*
55. Alma Stead, *Tupelo Daily Journal,* Nov 29, 1971.
56. The *Clarion-Ledger,* pg. 6, May 10,1979. The test was challenged in court as unfair, and an attempt to regulate the number of lawyers practicing in the state. The board of bar examiners ordered all failing papers in the Feb. 1978 bar exam re-evaluated, whereupon 65 additional law school grads were awarded passing scores. In view of the court challenge and adverse publicity, the legislature passed a bill in 1979 that would end the diploma privilege in 1984. Once Ole Miss Law School graduates were required to sit for a bar examination, the multi-state exam was chosen and passing percentages for all takers settled in the high to mid-eighties.
57. Note to the author, April 2010.
58. Note to the author, April 2010. Two papers from the class, submitted in open competition, were selected to be read before the Law Division, Association for Education in Journalism & Mass Communications.
59. Note to the author, May 2010.
60. Note to author, May 2010.
61. Note to the author, April 2010.
62. Hall, *Southern Scribe,* op. cit.
63. Ronald Farrar to Chancellor Porter L. Fortune, February 6, 1974.
64. Hoar, letter to University of Mississippi Director of Libraries, c. 1964.
65. Hoar, note to the author, c. 1985.
66. Hall, *Southern Scribe,* op. cit.
67. Quoted, The Mississippi Writer's Page website, August 1999.
68. ibid.
69. ibid.
70. *The Oxford Eagle,* September 30, 1994; Southern Scribe, op. cit., May 1,

2010.

71. Quoted in Mississippi Writers and Musicians web site, 2003.

S. Gale Denley

72. David Hitt, posted on his "All the World" blog, September 4, 2008.
73. *Calhoun County Journal*, et al., September 4, 2008.
74. *The Oxford Eagle*, November 15, 1996.
75. Mitchell to the author, November 5, 2010.
76. *The Oxford Eagle*, November 15, 1996.
77. *ibid.*
78. *ibid.*
79. *Calhoun County Journal*, September 3, 2008.

Will Norton

80. S. Gale Denley to the author c. 1983.
81. Note to the author, May 2010.
82. Note to the author, May 2010.
83. Note to the author, May 2010.
84. Jere Hoar to Gerald Walton, May 10, 1982.
85. Note to the author, March 2010.
86. Note to the author, May 2010.
87. Craft later became publisher of the *Jackson Sun* (TN) and the *Shreveport Journal*. Rose Jackson, an African American student from Clarksdale, won honors throughout her undergraduate years and in 1979 was named by *Glamour* magazine as one of the top 10 women college students in America. Sansing, *op. cit.*, 324.
88. Broadcasting had been present on the Ole Miss campus since the 1920s, initially under the Department of Physics and Astronomy, where it was studied for its technical and experimental possibilities.
89. Quoted in http://jackbass.com.
90. Note to the author, May 10, 2010.
91. Note to the author, May 11, 2010.
92. Note to the author, May 9, 2010.
93. Described more fully in the chapter dealing with student media.
94. Dunlap, op. cit., 83.
95. Dr. Husni's work is discussed more fully in the chapter, "Mr.Magazine."
96. Peter Wagner to Harvey Lewis, May 5, 1982.
97. Autry to Chancellor Fortune, June 2, 1982.

Don Sneed

98. Greenwood Publishing Co., 1991.
99. Department of Journalism, Annual Report, 1991-92.
100. *Editor & Publisher*, November 1, 2005, 9.
101. http://www.allbusiness.com, November 1, 2005.
102. *The Oxford Eagle*, c. June 1, 1993.
103. Jere Hoar to the author, June 4, 2010.
104. Gale Denley to the author, c. June 1996.
105. Interview with the author, June 29, 2010.
106. *ibid.*; also, *Editor & Publisher*, op. cit.

Stuart Bullion

107. Jere Hoar to the author, c. September 2010.
108. The *Clarion-Ledger*, May 14, 1997.
109. *The Oxford Eagle*, May 14, 1997.
110. *ibid.*
111. Bullion to Meek, May 6, 1997.
112. Hoar, interview with the author, October 2010.
113. Overby's assertion, which the chancellor found persuasive, was that the sparkling new Overby Center would make the aging Farley Hall, to which it would be attached, suffer by contrast.
114. The *Daily Mississippian*, c. May 10, 1997.
115. Elizabeth Shiver, interview with the author, November 11, 2010.
116. Hahn's engaging personality made her an ideal hostess for faculty and student social occasions.
117. Quoted in The *Daily Mississippian*, April 22, 2004.
118. These quotations from Bullion were printed in the program for his memorial service, April 30, 2004.
119. The *Daily Mississippian*, November 8, 1999.
120. *Bangor Daily News*, February 28, 1997.
121. Bullion entitled this essay "Why I Don't Like War Stories," but evidently never published it.
122. Wallace copied Bullion on his letter to the Provost, June 10, 2003.
123. Bullion to Provost Carolyn Ellis Staton, July 10, 2003.
124. Bullion to Dean Glenn Hopkins of the College of Liberal Arts, May 6, 2003.
125. The *Clarion-Ledger*, April 25, 2004.

Samir Husni

126. Susan Baker, "Embracing Childhood Passions: An Interview with

Samir Husni, aka 'Mr. Magazine,'" from *Spirit: A Magazine Designed for Diverse Women*, http://www.spirit.com (undated).

127. Robert T. Elson, *Atheneum*, 1968.
128. Norton, interviews with the author, Summer 2010.
129. Associated Press, "Mr. Magazine is a living museum of an ultra-competitive business," Quoted in *Tripoli-Lebanon.com*, posted December 23, 2002.
130. *Tripoli-Lebanon, op. cit.*
131. *ibid.*
132. Quoted in Husin's blog, *Mr. Magazine*, undated.
133. Interviews with the author, Summer 2010.
134. *Mr. Magazine, op. cit.*, June 11, 2010.
135. *ibid.*
136. Interviews with the author, Summer 2010.
137. *ibid.*
138. *ibid.;* interviews and correspondence with the author, Summer 2010, October 2011.

The Mississippi Scholastic Press Association

139. Forbes to Carolyn Heard McMillan, Quoted in *A History of the Mississippi Scholastic Press Association*, unpublished master's thesis, University of Mississippi (1985), 212.
140. *ibid.*, 3.
141. *ibid.*, 213.
142. *Tinker v. Des Moines Independent School District*, 393 U.S. 503 (1969).
143. S. Gale Denley and Ronald Farrar, "High School Journalists Are Worth Taking Seriously," *Bulletin of the American Society of Newspaper Editors* (July/August 1976), 11.
144. Thomas Engleman, Director of the Newspaper Fund, to Denley, October 1, 1968.
145. A list of Silver Em winners may be found in the Appendix II.
146. After her marriage to Dr. Will Norton.
147. Brenkert, *The Oxford Eagle*, March 22, 1984.
148. Bruce Konkle, interview with the author, September 6, 2010.

Student Media

149. Speech at 100th anniversary reunion of *Mississippian* staffers, June 17-18, 2011
150. Kincannon's defense of student freedom extended far beyond *The Mississippian*. Beset by a plethora of student disciplinary problems, real

and imagined, Kincannon resigned in 1914, stating that he was "unwilling to allow the University to become a political chattel." Quoted by Allen Cabiness, *The University of Mississippi: Its First Hundred Years*, 2d ed. (University Press of Mississippi, 1971), 128.

151. A source for much of this background is *100 Years of Mississippian Memories*, a publication for The Mississippian Centennial Celebration of and by former staff members in June, 2011. This excellent compilation was produced by Elizabeth Shiver, Prof. Pat Thompson and others.

152. The county where Starkville and Mississippi State are situated.

153. Address by Mississippi former Gov. William Winter at the Mississippian Centennial Celebration, *op. cit.*

154. *ibid.* It should be noted that Maralyn Howell's son, Stuart Bullion, would, many years later, be named chairman of the Ole Miss Department of Journalism.

155. Charles W. Eagles, *The Price of Defiance: James Meredith and the Integration of Ole Miss* (University of North Carolina Press, 2009),p. 60 *ff*.

156. Quoted by Otis R. Tims, "Standing by Its Principles," *Ole Miss Alumni Review*, March 1981, pp. 2-10.

157. Shiver, *op. cit.,* p. 37.

158. *ibid.*, p. 42

159. Karen Davis Hill ('69) note to the author, May 2010. Charles Overby's concern with editorial fairness to fraternities is noteworthy, since he was the first editor of *The Mississippian* who was not affiliated with a Greek society.

160. Eagles, *op. cit.*, p. 372.

161. A marker honoring Guihard was later placed outside the Journalism building.

162. *The Daily Mississippian*, October 1, 1962.

163. Sidna Brower Mitchell, note to the author, March 2011.

164. Tims, *op. cit.*

165. Shiver, *op. cit.,* p. 47

166. *ibid.,* p. 49.

167. Elijah Parish Lovejoy was a newspaper publisher in St. Louis and Alton, Ill., who was an outspoken abolitionist. A pro-slavery mob attacked his newspaper office and killed him in 1837, making him one of the earliest martyrs in the battle to end slavery.

168. Notes to the author, May-June 2010.

169. Tims, *op. cit.*

170. Quoted in Tims, *op. cit.* The origin of the poem is unattributed.

171. Much of this early background is drawn from Mary Wilhoit Harbour, *A History of the University of Mississippi Radio Station WCBH* (University of Mississippi, unpublished master's thesis, 1968.)

172. Broadcast rights for Ole Miss athletic events, always popular, by now had been sold to various commercial radio stations throughout the Mid-

South region.

173. *University of Mississippi Catalogue, 1950-51*, quoted by Harbour, *op. cit.*, p. 18.
174. Pratt was also something of a talent spotter. He once asked the department chairman to take note of a kid in his class that showed unusual promise. The student turned out to be Shepard Smith, who would win national acclaim as a prime-time anchor with Fox News.
175. Quoted in *The Oxford Eagle*, February 25, 2003.
176. Note to the author, May 2010. His students would challenge Braseth's modest self-characterization of being a "mediocre" teacher, arguing that he was far better than that.
177. Note to the author, May 2010.
178. Note to the author, June 2010.
179. David Sansing, *The University of Mississippi: A Sesquicentennial History* (Jackson: University Press of Mississippi, 1999) p. 167.
180. *ibid.*
181. From a profile written by Jack Bales, *Mississippi Writer's Page* web site, undated.
182. *The Ole Miss Magazine*, December, 1981, p. 6.
183. A nationally prominent leader in the civil rights movement.
184. "Hanging Tough," in *Whatever Happened to Main Street?* published by the Ed and Becky Meek School of Journalism and New Media, November 2011, p. 6.

Ed Meek

185. Jere Hoar to the author, August 2010.
186. This background is drawn from interviews and other communications with the author, during the summer of 2010.
187. John Meek eventually transferred to Mississippi College, a Baptist school, and went on to carve out a distinguished career in the ministry.
188. Meek's photograph of Meredith was chosen for the cover of *The Price of Defiance: James Meredith and the Integration of Ole Miss*, by Dr. Charles W. Eagles (North Carolina: 2009), the definitive treatment of the Meredith story.
189. 359 F2d 994 (1966)
190. Note to the author, March 2010.
191. Note to the author, March 2010.
192. Note to the author, March 2010.
193. Note to the author, March 2010.
194. Note to the author, March 2010.
195. Miss Hamblett's work is famous not only for the pictures she painted, but for how she painted them. Each of her paintings is done from a child's

point of view. The Ogden Museum of Southern Art in New Orleans is a rich source of background material on her and her work.

The Meek School Era Begins

196. Information provided by the University of Mississippi Public Affairs Department.
197. Khayat, interview with the author, March 17, 2010.
198. *ibid*.
199. *The Oxford Eagle,* October 19, 2009.
200. Angela Moore Atkins, "Changing Times", *Ole Miss Alumni Magazine*, Winter 2010, 26-27.
201. The "interim" title was removed during one of these.
202. Atkins, *op. cit.*
203. Interview with the author, May 14, 2010.
204. *Meek School Administrative Report, 2010.*
205. Simon & Schuster, 2001.
206. Crown Publishers, 2010. The book's subtitle is *Scruggs' Ambition for Ecuador.*
207. Note to the author, February 10, 2010.
208. Note to the author, March 1, 2010.
209. A complete list of the Meek School's faculty and staff may be found in the Appendix.
210. At the commencement ceremony each graduate was presented with a lavishly printed copy of the First Amendment to the United States Constitution: "Congress shall make no law respecting an establishment of religion, or prohibiting the free exercise thereof; or abridging the freedom of speech, or of the press, or of the right of the people peaceably to assemble, and to petition the government for a redress of grievances."

Photo by Katherine Williamson

Appendix I

Faculty and Staff
2014

The following composed the faculty and staff of the Ed and Becky Meek School of Journalism and New Media in 2013.

Will Norton, Jr. - Professor and Dean, Ph. D. University of Iowa.

Charles D. Mitchell - Assistant Dean, J.D. University of Mississippi School of Law.

Jeanni Atkins - Associate Professor, Ph.D., University of Missouri.

Joseph B. Atkins - Professor, M.A., American University, Washington, D.C.

Thomas Chapman - Manager of Media Technology, Student Media Center

Mark K. Dolan - Associate Professor, Ph.D., University of South Carolina.

Nancy McKenzie Dupont - Associate Professor, Ph.D., University of Southern Mississippi.

Scott Fiene - Assistant Professsor, M.A., Drake University

Roy Frostenson - Assistant Director of Student Media, Student Media Center

Vanessa Gregory - Assistant Professor, M.A., University of California-Berkeley.

Mikki Harris - Assistant Professor, M.A., Boston University

Samir A. Husni - Professor and Hederman Lecturer, Director of the Magazine Innovation Center. Ph.D., University of Missouri.

Deidre Jackson - Instructor. B. A., Mississippi University for Women.

Darrel Jordan - Chief Engineer, M.A., University of Mississippi.

Robert Magee - Assistant Professor, Ph.D., University of North Carolina at Chapel Hill

Ellen Meacham - Instructor. M.A., University of Mississippi.

Mykki Newton - Videographer/Editor. M.F.A., University of Mississippi.

Debra Novak - Creative Services Manager, Student Media Center

Evangeline Robinson - Assistant Professor, M.A. University of Mississippi

Bill Rose - Adjunct Instructor. B. A., University of Mississippi.

Darren Sanefski - Assistant Professor, M.A., Syracuse University.

Bradley E. Schultz - Associate Professor, Ph.D. Texas Tech University.
Chris Canty Sparks - Assistant Professor, MBA Vanderbilt University
Alysia Steele - Assistant Professor, M.A., Ohio University.
Robin Street - Lecturer. M.A., M.S., University of Mississippi.
Kristen Alley Swain - Assistant Professor, Ph.D., University of Florida.
Patricia Thompson - Assistant Professor and Director of Student Media. B.J., University of Missouri.

Deborah Halpern Wenger - Assistant Professor. M.A., University of North Carolina--Charlotte.

Kathleen Woodruff Wickham - Associate Professor. Ed.D., University of Memphis.

Curtis Wilkie - Associate Professor, Overby Fellow. B.A., University of Mississippi.

Appendix II

Silver Em Recipients

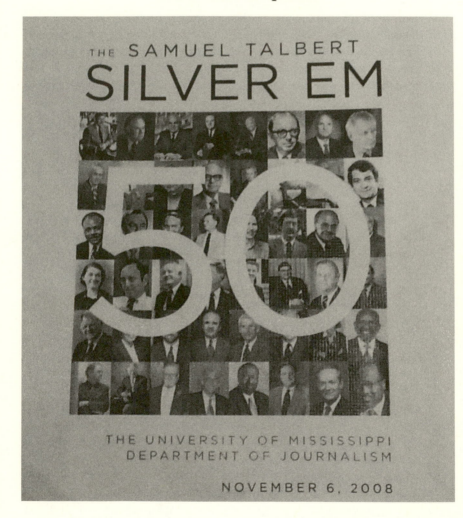

The following were named to receive the Silver Em, renamed in more recent years the Samuel Talbert Silver Em Award. Recipients are Mississippians with remarkable careers in the media, in or out of the state, or media professionals who worked all or most of their careers in Mississippi.

1958 – George W. Healy Jr.
1959 – Turner Catledge
1960 – Kenneth Toler
1961 – John Oliver Emmerich
1963 – George McLean
1964 – William B. Street
1965 – Purser Hewitt
1966 – Hal C. DeCell
1967 – Paul Pittman
1968 – Hodding Carter Jr.
1969 – Willie Morris
1970 – T.M. Hederman Jr.
1971 – Joseph R. Ellis
1972 – Wilson F. Minor
1973 – Mark F. Ethridge
1975 – H.L. Stevenson
1976 – William Raspberry
1977 – Joe L. Albritton
1978 – James A. Autry
1979 – James Nelson
1980 – Mary-Lynn Kotz
1981 – Curtis Wilkie
1982 – Harold Burson
1983 – John O. Emmerich
1984 – Hazel Brannon Smith
1985 – Charles Overby
1986 – W.C. "Dub" Shoemaker
1987 – Charles Dunagin
       Larry Speakes
1988 – Edward Fritts
1989 – Rudy Abramson
1990 – Hodding Carter III
1991 – James L. McDowell
1992 – Rheta Grimsley Johnson
1993 – Dan Goodgame
1994 – Robert Gordon
1995 – Jere Hoar
1996 – Gregory Favre
1997 – Stephanie Saul
1998 – Lerone Bennett
2000 – Jerry Mitchell
2001 – Bert Case
2002 – Ira Harkey

2003 – Jim Abbott
2005 – Otis Sanford
2006 – Dan Phillips
2007 – Stanley Dearman
2008 – Ronnie Agnew
2009 – Stan Tiner
2010 – Terry Wooten
2011 – Patsy Brumfield
2012 – Greg Brock
2013 – Randall Pinkston

Appendix III

Board of Visitors
2014

James A. Autry, author, poet and former magazine publishing executive at the Meredith Corporation.

Harold Burson, former CEO of Burson-Marstellar and Associates.

Harold Crump, former broadcasting executive who retired from Hubbard Broadcasting in 2013.

Eddie Fritts, former executive director of the National Association of Broadcasters.

Mary Lynn Kotz, author from the Washington, D.C., metropolitan area.

Ed Meek, media leader and public relations executive.

Charles Overby, former vice president of news for the Gannett Co., Inc., and former CEO of the Freedom Forum.

Susanne Shaw, Professor at the University of Kansas and executive director of the Accrediting Council on Education in Journalism and Mass Communications.

Dub Shoemaker, former reporter for the *Jackson Daily News* and publisher of *The Star Herald,* Kosciusko, MS.

Richard Starmann, former Senior Officer of Worldwide Communications at McDonald's Corporation.

Blake Tartt III, President and Chief Executive Officer of New Regional Planning and an urban developer with a unique blend of social, design and financial acumen.

John B. Thomas, former Vice President of Investor Relations and Public Affairs for Abbott and President of the Abbott Fund.

Appendix IV

Ole Miss Journalism Enrollment Figures 1978-2013

Fall Semester	Journalism Bachelors	Masters	Journalism & Advertising Bachelors	Masters	Radio & TV Bachelors	Masters	Marketing Communications Bachelors	Masters
1978	178	0	0	0	150	0	0	0
1979	226	0	0	0	190	0	0	0
1980	381	0	0	0	8	0	0	0
1981	189	6	57	0	69	3	0	0
1982	176	15	62	0	77	1	0	0
1983	Data not available						0	0
1984	154	17	54	0	69	1	0	0
1985	134	13	50	0	81	1	0	0
1986	129	18	63	0	86	0	0	0
1987	180	16	56	0	57	0	0	0
1988	210	27	58	0	43	0	0	0
1989	243	40	54	0	35	0	0	0
1990	Data not available						0	0
1991	255	36	56	0	55	0	0	0
1992	230	46	45	0	42	0	0	0
1993	246	40	41	0	51	0	0	0
1994	227	33	40	0	54	0	0	0
1995	223	33	40	0	54	0	0	0
1996	217	30	39	0	62	0	0	0
1997	192	27	28	0	85	0	0	0

Fall	Journalism		Journalism & Advertising		Radio & TV		Marketing Communications	
Semester	Bachelors	Masters	Bachelors	Masters	Bachelors	Masters	Bachelors	Masters
1999	204	18	31	0	74	0	0	0
2000	233	14	9	0	80	0	0	0
2001	336	18	7	0	42	0	28	0
2002	346	25	2	0	16	0	89	0
2003	340	18	0	0	17	0	128	0
2004	315	19	0	0	1	0	139	0
2005	393	25	0	0	0	0	159	0
2006	453	36	0	0	0	0	172	0
2007	448	24	0	0	0	0	185	0
2008	495	21	0	0	0	0	192	0
2009	511	22	0	0	0	0	194	0
2010	501	26	0	0	0	0	179	0
2011	572	14	0	0	0	0	216	0
2012	544	25	0	0	0	0	167	0
2013	479	33	0	0	0	0	408	0

Appendix V

Gerald Forbes Interview

March 22, 1984

"The students that put out the high school paper are the brightest kids in the school. It's almost invariable. They are the brightest kids- whatever they're interested in.

"Well- I wanted to get all of them that I could into the journalism department. Not just into the department, but into the University of Mississippi.

"So I started the Press Institute which didn't tell anybody anything much. But the kids loved to come, and we put on a dance and a dinner and finally got a little contest into it, with some sort of semi-honors that we passed around. That pleased the teachers, and it pleased the kids."

So you founded the Press Institute?
Sure.

What purpose did you have in mind when you established it?
To attract the high school students. I did the Press Institute my first year here.

What activities were included in the first Press Institute?
We had a dance and a dinner. It used to be in the main dining room of the Cafeteria, and that got crowded.

There was great difficulty taking care of the high school kids.

What time of the year was the Press Institute held?
I held it in the spring, when school was gonna be out.

What sessions were included?
I don't remember any programs.

How were schools contacted?
That wasn't hard to do- just write a letter to the superintendent. If you got a reply, you had it made.

How often did you contact them?
Oh- when we were getting ready to have one of these sessions- that was all.

How was the press institute funded?
Papa and Mama sent the kids- those were all the funds there were.

How much did it cost them to attend?
I don't know what it cost them- some of them spent a lot of money, and some of them never. I guess I don't know. The University didn't spend any joney on them. The University helped out with the Cafeteria and the dinner and the dance.

We always had a dance for these kids, in the gymnasium.
I remember we had to hire a band or dance orchestra-
whatever they called that. We'd get two or three women to
chaperone, but that was never any particular difficulty.
The only time anything unthwarted happened was at a dance
and it was supposed to end at 11 o'clock, which sounds pretty
early, but then on the other hand, I was dealing with a
bunch of high school kids, from heaven-knows-whose-home,
you see. The boy who was leading the dance-"The orgesa"
- the Orgesa was a bunch of University boys- wouldn't stop.
I told him 'Look, it's 11:00- it's time to stop, and he just
goes tootin' along. Pretty soon I lost my temper. We
might've had a real messy time, but then he quit. And
that's the only time we ever had any kind of difficulty
with the dance. The youngsters loved it.

Was there a coordinator or secretary of the Press Institute?
     Heavens no. It was all part of my job. There were a
few occasional teachers who got her nose out of joint because
junior didn't win a prize or something, but I always managed
to get around that by giving them another prize when I found
out she was disturbed. You've got to have the high school
teachers with you at a thing like that.

Did you have any problems with Continuing Education?
     Didn't have any continuing education. This was before
there was anything like that. They built a building then,
but that was all.

Who wrote the Press Institute Constitution?
     There wasn't any Constitution. Whatever Constitution
there was was in my head. You may have a dozen Constitutions
now, but we didn't have any.

Was The Journalist published?
     No. They just came up here for the joy-ride- and a lot
of them liked it well enough to come back and enroll.

Were contests held for the high school students?
     No- not exactly. We didn't have anything that was known
as a contest. We didn't call it a contest. Of course there
was- there is- contesting all of the time, but it wasn't any
organized contest.

You said that some students won awards?
     Oh well- you know- Miss Josephine Link has to take
something home to brag about. Well, you better give something
to Josephine Link to brag about. Now that's the kind of
awards there were. I probably did that in sort of an
underhanded way.

<u>Was it considered desirable that every school win an award?</u>
Oh no- if they weren't really mad, we didn't have
any awards, that is- there weren't any specific cups or
anything of that kind- we just declared that so and so was
the best delegation, or something like that.

<u>So you decided that?</u>
Yeah- I didn't say I did, but that's about the way it
happened.

<u>Were there schools that consistently won awards from year</u>
<u>to year?</u>
No -- oh no. Nothing like that. It was always someone
different. If you're gonna get any publicity, the same guy
can't get it all the time.

<u>MSPA Questions</u>

<u>1. What would you think the principal goal of MSPA should</u>
<u>be?</u>
Well- you could have had two or three principal goals,
it seems to me. One of the goals could be to really teach
them some journalism, so they could go to work on a newspaper. But that would be pretty difficult, because it takes
more training and time and study than a high school student
wants to give. But that could be a good goal.
Our purpose was simply to build a following for the
department of journalism. I think we succeeded. But- it's
the kind of a nebulus thing that you can't quite put your
finger on. But I think we succeeded. I think the department
of journalism got quite a lot of prestige with the high school
kids.
And they did come. And the department of journalism is
growing like everything and I think they knew of it because
of the beginning of the Press Institute. Now that's only
my assumption, and I don't know a whole lot about what I'm
talking about because it's been so many years since I was in
any way involved with the Press Institute.

<u>3. What would be three duties you see as most important</u>
<u>for a person responsible for the department's MSPA work?</u>
Well, for one thing, they must believe in what they're
doing. That is about the first thing. You've got to
believe you're doing something that is worthwhile and should
be done. And Talbert and I certainly felt that way about
the Department of Journalism. That would be one thing.
How well they can pass that idea on is something else.
Some people would go for it, and some wouldn't.

4. What characteristics would you think are most important
in any employee responsible for working with high school
students and advisers? Please rank them:
1. Professional Experience
2. Vigor and Energy
3. Teaching experience
4. Youth, and the ability to empathize

5. How important to the department of journalism should
be the teaching function of MSPA in comparison with the
recruiting function?
     I'd be kind of hesitant to say the recruiting ought to
be any function. I think the people who come and get involved
ought to do that all on their own. If it isn't voluntary,
it won't have very much spirit to it. If it's something
a kid wants to do and he's doing it because he enjoys it,
o.k., he'll do a much better job and there isn't really any
way I know you can get someone to do that.
     I think about all MSPA can do for the University is to
bring students to the university- whatever they teach. And
of course, in this particular instance, the thing MSPA is
interested in is a student to be journalism oriented.

9. How valuable do you think reasonably well conducted
workshops throughout the state would be to bring about the
goals you previously noted for the Association?
     Well, they'd be expensive. That's one thing. If you
can get the funds to do it, well that would be just fine.
But I think the goal would be kind of hard to discern--
in other words, just what did you accomplish? It would be
very valuable to some of the students- some of the others
would love to come, but they couldn't learn anything.

10. Did you have student officers?
     Oh yeah- I think they had some officers. But that
was just theoretical. They didn't really function as
officers.

How could more use have been made of them?
     I don't know if we were in any position to make any more
use of them, because you have to bear in mind, this was a
very nebulous organization. Basically, it depended on me.
I ran the blooming show. Maybe apparently, and maybe no-
one knew it, but I did.

I can remember some 45 or 50 year old high school teacher
who was so angry that she had tears in her eyes, because
little junior hadn't gotten some sort of something. By
golly, I corrected that right away. I know that what I'm
telling you happened, but I can't remember the details
of it. And she went home just happy as the dickens with
something to give to the newspaper about what they'd done
here. It's a public relations affair, too.

11. What could teacher officers do that might help MSPA?
     I'd be kind of slow about pushing it very hard, because
most of the high school teachers have got more than they've
got time to do anyway. Somebody's always wanting them to
add just a little bit more, and to do this or that. When
you add it all together, the poor girl is distracted. In
most cases they simply don't have the time to do anything
else.

Appendix VI

Fran Talbert Interview
(Mrs. Sam Talbert)

Interview with Mrs ∧ Talbert (Fran)
Sam

April 2, 1984

<u>Did your husband run the Press Institute, or did someone else?</u>
He did it, at first. And then I think there were some years when Gail helped him. But that was one of his prime things- especially at first. And then the Continuing Education helped him with some of these details in later years.

<u>Did he have any trouble with Continuing Ed?</u>
They helped a lot with the footwork and housing. I really can't even recall when that took place and when ᵛontinuing Ed. took over. I recall when children were staying in the gym.
It was a full 2 days-- I think they were here 2 nights possibly. At least one night. They'd come in for a full day and have the night and the next day-- but it was always a big dance. That was over early. They also served a banquet in the early stages of it. The Cafeteria catered that. It would be in the Old Gum, and that's where the dances were. And then later, they moved it over to the Alumni House (they moved Cont. Ed. over there) and they would have skits that they performed. For this evening of entertainment, they would have the banquet and then the dance and then the different schools performed skits and it'd be competition which had a lot of involvement in that.

<u>Do you remember where the students stayed?</u>
Yes. Early on, at the very beginning, the girls all stayed at the Education Gym, and the boys at the Gym on the campus. They'd bring their own sheets and pillows. It was dorm style. I recall that was a big thing-- getting sponsors to spend the night with them--you know, really, we treated them as high school children. Then, later, they moved over into empty dorms for a year or two. There was housing for the sponsors at the alumni house. Now I have no idea where it went from there, really.

<u>Do you remember why it stopped being a two-day thing?</u>
I don't know--that would be after Sam died. That'd be 12 years ago. I get the feeling it's only a one day thing now.

I can remember a group getting together when they were critiquing the papers and judging the papers. As far as the judging of the paper and the yearbooks, Taylor Publishing Co. used to always do it and the <u>Commercial Appeal</u> staff always was very active in it. The Memphis Advertising Association and WMT Radio, also. It seems to have branched out to a wider area, but there was always just very big news articles in the Commercial all during the Press Institute. Then, I think possibly, there was a lot of advance publicity. But anyway, the people of Memphis were most supportive of all of this.

194

<u>Was the Journalist published?</u>
Yes.

<u>How did Dr. Talbert view the Press Institute?</u>
He thought it was one of the most important things that
they were doing--stimulating young journalists.

<u>What was his main objective?</u>
To <u>teach</u> them of journalism. To make the school papers
very effective. He always believed and knew that some of the
brightest students were those that were writing for the paper
and were deep into journalism.
He never felt that was a burden. He felt that was a very
important part of their duties to Mississippi.

<u>Silver Em:</u>

I remember when the Silver Em was instituted. Chancellor
Williams at that time felt that they should do something for
the Mississippians and he approached Sam about this. This idea
came up, to honor an outstanding journalist with Mississippi
background. I recall so well the time Mr. Healy got it and he
was unable to come. At the time, they wanted to give them
something different than an ordinary plaque. I think now they
give them a plaque. Sam thought it would be very meaningful if
some of the local talent did it. The first one was a ceramic
plate. (1963) This one may be the last one they had done like
this. At the time this was presented, they held the awards
over in the Education Building in the Auditorium, because there
was such a large crowd.
I know Sam had so much trouble with these. They wouldn't
get them done, or they wouldn't turn out right. I believe
that's when they went to the Plaque. They thought it was more
meaningful that it came from this kind of an institute--young
people who recognized the ability that had come from --.

<u>Golden Em:</u>
The Gold Em was originally started for my husband. That was
to have been a surprise for Sam that year--all these years they
had given the Silver Em award . Then they wanted to give Sam
one. They were gonna surprise him--he had been quite ill, but
then he died 5 days before the award was given. They brought
it over here to my home.

(The em is symbolism in the old print shop. It was more
meaningful to journalists because of the em=-- that made it
distinctive.

195

Acknowledgments

When Will Norton and Ed Meek contacted me, an old friend who had long since retired and lived in far-away South Carolina, to ask that I write a history of journalism at the University of Mississippi, I felt obliged to point out a couple of things:

1. Since I had chaired that very program many, many years ago I could hardly be objective in describing it. To the contrary, they said, the program has come a long, long way since then. (As indeed it has.) Besides, my early experience at Ole Miss would give me a better context for understanding the dramatic extent of growth and change from the days when I was there more than 30 years earlier.

2. That they, Will Norton and Ed Meek, would inevitably emerge as two of the heroes in the story, a characterization that neither man, modest and self-deprecatory, would relish. To this they argued that I would find that the real heroes of the story would be the students, the young men and women who had gone through the program, and who possessed the smarts and the grit to carve out amazingly successful careers for themselves in the high-profile, hotly competitive field of mass communications.

They were right, of course. I discovered that this story indeed has many heroes (and heroines). Others can judge how objectively they have been portrayed in these pages.

The book was not an easy one to write, separated as I was by so much distance and so many years, and doing it at all would not have been possible without help. Fortunately I had a great deal of it. Jace Ponder, then a graduate student, proved to be a tireless research assistant, wise well beyond his years and extraordinarily quick on the uptake. Dr. Jere Hoar, a friend and former colleague, not only knew the history of journalism at Ole Miss, but he lived it and helped shape it. In his attic were boxes of papers he had kept over the years, materials that provided detail and insight available nowhere else, and I am grateful that he generously shared these files with me. Another splendid source was Elizabeth Shiver. One of the earliest graduates in journalism at Ole Miss, Liz attained considerable success in journalism and public relations, much of the time living and working in Washington. When she moved back to Oxford, she was prevailed upon to serve on the journalism Advisory Committee, and not much happens in Oxford or at Ole Miss that escapes her notice. Enduringly interested in the program, Liz gave direction to the highly successful Centennial Celebration of the *Mississippian*, a paper she once edited. Like Jere Hoar, Liz possesses a wonderful ability to recall events and to explain them in interesting and precise detail. Conversations with them, and there were quite a few, were not only convivial but informative.

Special thanks to my daughter, Janet Farrar Worthington, for her editorial skills and enthusiastic encouragement. Help came from many other sources as well, particularly from current and former top administrators of the university, faculty members including Charlie Mitchell, publisher Larry Wells of Yoknapatawpha Press, Susan Norton, Kathy Ferguson, Katie Williamson, and Sam Talbert's children—Mary, Pat, Suzanne and Mike—who kindly provided photographs, letters and newspaper clippings. I would especially like to thank Bill Rose for his counsel and support. He is a gifted journalist who was a top editor at the *Miami Herald* and the *Palm Beach Post* before joining the faculty at the Meek School.

One final observation: Before agreeing to undertake this project, I confess to having had mixed feelings about it. On the plus side, I looked forward to reconnecting again with Oxford and Ole Miss, where my family and I had spent four happy years long ago. But I had to share with Will and Ed my doubts that anybody would be interested in the story of one relatively small academic unit in one Deep South university. Don't worry about it, they said, the story will be bigger and more important than you think. Turns out they were right about that, too.

–Ronald Farrar
Columbia, South Carolina, November 2011